80 DELICIOUS RECIPES YOU'LL CO

Just for One or Two

D*a*IRY COOKBOOK

Contents

Introduction	4
Everyday Eating	8
Serves 1	10
Serves 2	34
Eat & Freeze	60
Eat Out, In	120
Serves 1	122
Serves 2	136

Cooking in small quantities can seem like too much effort, with lots of preparation for just one or two meals, and most recipes catering for four or more people.

This book, however, is different. It shows you how to cook delicious meals for one or two people with readily available ingredients, little effort and minimal waste.

The Recipes

The book is split into three chapters – Everyday Eating, Eat & Freeze and Eat Out, In.

Everyday Eating
Introduces you to a whole host of fabulous everyday meals that use storecupboard ingredients plus a few fresh foods. They are simple to cook and easy enough to make at any time. The chapter is split into two with the first half dedicated to recipes for one person (but easy to double up for two) and the second half providing recipes for two.

Eat & Freeze
In the Eat & Freeze chapter each recipe provides several portions so that you can create meals in advance. Eat one portion and freeze the rest for instant future dinners.

Eat Out, In
The Eat Out, In chapter is perfect for when you fancy something a little more special as it shows you how to create delicious restaurant-quality food at home with a few choice ingredients and little effort.

The recipes have been designed to have minimal leftovers. Where they do have any leftovers, they are mostly long-life ingredients, which will keep for several weeks or longer.

In the cook's tips you will find handy hints and helpful suggestions for leftovers. All the recipes have been triple-tested to ensure that they work perfectly every time.

 Many recipes are suitable for **freezing**; look out for the symbol and the Eat & Freeze chapter.

V This symbol flags recipes that are suitable for **vegetarians**. Use cheese or yogurt that is vegetarian-friendly.

Nutritional information is per portion/item and is based on the higher number (e.g. if it makes 10-12 biscuits, the calories are based on 12). The analyses don't include serving suggestions.

The QR code under the ingredients list can be scanned with your smartphone to provide you with a handy shopping list. The list is embedded in the QR code so no internet access is required.

Shop Wisely

With many supermarkets offering large packs of ingredients, shopping for one or two can be tricky. Be savvy and you can buy exactly what you need, reduce food waste and save money too.

- Peruse your cupboards and fridge and plan your meals for the week, using up any ingredients you have first. Make a list of the ingredients you need for the remaining meals.

- Stick to your shopping list.

- If you are tempted by multi-buy deals ensure that it is something you can store for a while, or freeze. Separate into portions, seal and store appropriately.

- Check use-by dates before you buy.

- Buy fresh produce loose, rather than in large packs. When buying fruit, choose a selection of ripe and unripe.

- Purchase meat and fish from the butcher/fishmonger or supermarket counter so that you can request exactly what you need for each recipe.

- Organise your fridge with the items with the shortest date at the front.

- Use your freezer! It's a small householder's best friend (see overleaf for more info).

Be Freezer Friendly

The freezer can be incredibly useful for a small household – for ready-frozen items such as peas and other vegetables, as well as fish and meat and make-ahead meals.

Many foods can be frozen to prolong their shelf life significantly. See the list of foods on the opposite page for a general guide on what you can freeze. Always check the label, freeze by its use-by date, and don't freeze if it says the item has been previously frozen.

Ensure any cooked foods are completely cold before freezing and always freeze in individual portions. Wrap the food well; store in a plastic tub with a tight-fitting lid or in a well-sealed bag. Squeeze out all the air and label with the date and foodstuff using a permanent pen.

Try eating from the freezer at least once a week so that the carefully frozen food doesn't lie untouched for months. Place the frozen tub or bag(s) in a bowl in the fridge overnight to thaw completely. Then decant into the bowl or a pan and heat gently in the microwave or on the hob until it is piping hot.

Ingredients Suitable for Freezing

Biscuits
Bought biscuits keep well in an airtight tin but homemade biscuits can be frozen before they're cooked.

Bread
Leave in its original packaging unless it's wrapped in paper, then transfer to a polythene bag.

Butter
Leave in its original packaging.

Cake
Most cakes freeze well but sponge cakes are better frozen before they are filled.

Cheese
Grate hard cheese before freezing and cut soft cheese into portions; don't freeze cottage cheese or Mozzarella.

Chestnuts
Freeze whole in polythene bags.

Chillies
Freeze whole in polythene bags.

Coffee (fresh beans or ground)
Freeze in its vacuum-packed bag.

Croissants
Freeze in a single layer before sealing in a polythene bag.

Fish
Check it's not been previously frozen, separate into portions, then wrap well.

Fruit
Open-freeze raw fruit in a single layer on a tray then pop into a polythene bag; freeze cooked fruit in plastic tubs.

Fruit juice
Freeze in the carton.

Gravy
Freeze in ice cube trays.

Herbs
Freeze whole sprigs in polythene bags; store chopped herbs in small tubs.

Home-cooked meals
Many can be frozen, especially casseroles, curries and bakes, though rice and pasta dishes don't work so well; check recipes for ❻.

Milk
Freeze in a plastic container.

Meat
Raw or cooked meat freezes well; remove any fat, separate into portions, then wrap well.

Pancakes
Interleave with baking paper, then pop into a polythene bag.

Pastry
Wrap raw pastry well in useful-sized portions.

Pies
Can be frozen raw or cooked, wrapped in polythene bags.

Puddings
Many can be frozen; see Eat & Freeze.

Quiches and tarts
Freeze cooked in polythene bags.

Sauces
Pour into small tubs or ice cube trays.

Soups
Pour into a rigid container.

Vegetables
Peel and chop, blanch in hot water for 2 minutes, then plunge into cold water, drain, dry then freeze.

Yogurt
Freeze in the sealed tub.

Yorkshire Pudding
Freeze in polythene bags.

Everyday Eating

Mozzarella & Asparagus Baguette	10	
Parmesan Plaice	13	
Pappardelle with Chorizo-Topped Cod	14	
Grilled Mackerel with Hot Cabbage Salad	17	
Potted Shrimps	18	
Chicken Goujons with Pea Shoot Salad	21	
Southern-Style Chicken with Oven-Baked Chips	22	
Pancetta Omelette with Pea Shoot Salad	25	
Pancetta & Mushrooms on Toast with Egg	26	
Pan-Fried Pork with Homemade Spicy Beans	29	
Roast Beef in a Yorkshire Pudding	30	
Italian Meatballs	33	
Griddled Halloumi with Wild Rocket	34	
Romano Peppers Stuffed with Fruity Couscous	37	
Vegetable Chow Mein	38	
Goat's Cheese & Mushroom Pizza	41	
Hearty Kiln-Roasted Salmon Salad	42	
Baked Salmon Tricolore	45	
Prawn & Mango Curry	46	
Spiced Chicken on a Bun	49	
Thai Chicken Skewers	50	
Chicken Escalopes with Thyme and Courgette	53	
Stir-Fried Pork with Egg-Fried Rice	54	
Spicy Lamb with Creamy Mash	57	
Cheat's Beef Curry	58	

Serves 1

Mozzarella & Asparagus Baguette

Time 25 minutes
Per portion: 680 Kcal
36g fat (11g saturated)

Ready-to-bake baguette 1 small

Asparagus spears 3, depending on size, woody ends snapped off then halved

Mayonnaise 1 tbsp

Finely shredded basil 1 tbsp

Finely chopped parsley 1 tbsp

Tomato 1, sliced

Mozzarella cheese 50g (2oz), thinly sliced

Freshly ground black pepper

 Scan the **QR Code** with a smartphone for an ingredients shopping list

To cook the baguette, preheat the oven according to the packet's instructions and bake the baguette. Remove it from the oven and set aside to cool.

Meanwhile, cook the asparagus spears in gently boiling, lightly salted water for 3–5 minutes until tender. Drain.

Cut the baguette almost into two lengthways. Mix the mayonnaise with the basil and parsley and spread over the cut sides of the baguette.

Lay alternate slices of tomato, Mozzarella and pieces of asparagus on the baguette. Season with pepper and serve immediately.

 This is a great way to use leftover herbs; chop and mix any herbs you have to hand with the mayonnaise.

You can use any cheese of your choice.

Colourful and simple, this delicious baguette provides a filling lunch and is a great way to use up leftover herbs and cheeses.

Ready in just ten minutes, but packed full of flavour, this pan-fried fish dish is perfect for a speedy weekday dinner.

Parmesan Plaice

 Serves 1

Time 10 minutes
Per portion: 457 Kcal
22g fat (7g saturated)

Mix together the flour, salt and pepper and sprinkle on a plate. Beat the egg in a wide shallow bowl and stir in the sage.

Coat the fish fillets in the flour, then dip them in the beaten egg and finally coat in cheese.

Heat the oil in a pan, fry the fish, skin-side up for a minute then flip the fillets and fry for about 1 more minute until cooked through and tender.

Serve on a plate with salad or green beans and new potatoes, if using.

Plain flour 2 tsp

Salt and freshly ground black pepper

Egg 1

Chopped sage leaves 1 tsp

Plaice fillets 2
(about 130g/4½oz each)

Grated Parmesan cheese
4 tbsp

Olive oil 2 tsp

Salad or green beans to serve (optional)

New potatoes to serve (optional)

Scan the **QR Code** with a smartphone for an ingredients shopping list

Plaice fillets are fabulous cooked like this but you could try lemon sole for a treat. It may need 1 more minute to cook.

You won't use all the beaten egg, but you could add some sweetcorn to the remaining mix and make a little fritter.

Serves 1

Pappardelle with Chorizo-Topped Cod

Time 10 minutes
Per portion: 562 Kcal
24g fat (6g saturated)

Dried pappardelle or fettucine 50g (2oz)

Green beans 50g (2oz), halved

Salt and freshly ground black pepper

Thick cod fillet or haddock 150g (5oz)

Olive oil 1 tsp

Chorizo 3–4 thin slices

Cherry tomatoes 65g (2½oz), halved

Chopped basil 1 tbsp

 Scan the QR Code with a smartphone for an ingredients shopping list

Preheat the grill to hot with the rack about 10cm (4in) away from the heat. Put a baking sheet underneath to heat up.

Add the pappardelle or fettucine to a pan of boiling water and bring back to the boil. Simmer for 5 minutes then add the beans and cook for 5 minutes until the pasta is al dente.

While the pasta is cooking, season the fish and drizzle it with a little oil. Arrange the chorizo slices, overlapping, on top. Transfer the fish to the hot tray with the tomatoes and grill for 3–5 minutes until the fish is cooked through.

Drain the pasta and beans and toss with the basil in a warmed bowl. Lay the fish on top of the pasta with the tomatoes. Drizzle with a little more oil if you like.

Instead of beans, you could try tenderstem broccoli, asparagus tips, shredded runner beans or samphire (just cook the last two options for 1–2 minutes with the pasta).

For an extra flavour boost, dot the finished dish with some ready-made pesto.

Ready-sliced chorizo that is well wrapped keeps for a couple of weeks in the fridge. Crisp slices in a pan to add to stir fries, omelettes or scrambled egg or on top of mash or baked beans.

Packed full of classic Mediterranean flavours, this scrumptious dish of fish, chorizo, pasta and veg will make you feel as though you're holidaying somewhere sunny.

Vibrant red cabbage adds wonderful colour to this autumnal dish. The anise-like taste of caraway complements the soft oily fish.

Grilled Mackerel with Hot Cabbage Salad

 Serves 1

Time 10 minutes
Per portion: 401 Kcal
25g fat (5g saturated)

Preheat the grill to hot.

Season the fish with salt and pepper and place on a sheet of oiled foil in the base of a grill pan. Grill for 8–10 minutes, turning once, until browned and the flesh flakes when pressed with a knife.

Meanwhile, to make the salad, heat the oil in a non-stick frying pan. Add the onion and cabbage, toss together and fry for 5 minutes, stirring once or twice.

Stir in the apple, caraway seeds, vinegar, sugar and a little salt and pepper. Cover and fry for 3–4 minutes until the cabbage is tender.

Spoon the cabbage and apple mix onto a warmed plate and top with the mackerel. Serve with crusty bread if you wish.

Mackerel 2 fillets
Salt and freshly ground black pepper
Sunflower oil 1 tsp
Onion 1 small, peeled and sliced
Red cabbage 75g (3oz), finely shredded
Dessert apple 1, peeled, cored and chopped
Caraway seeds ¼ tsp
Vinegar 1 tsp
Soft light brown sugar 1 tsp
Crusty bread to serve (optional)

 Scan the **QR Code** with a smartphone for an ingredients shopping list

 Cook's TIPS

If you like, you can buy boneless ready-cooked mackerel fillets and omit steps 1 and 2.

Instead of the caraway seeds you could use cinnamon for a spicy-sweet flavour. Use any leftover cabbage to make a crunchy red coleslaw or cook slowly with water, butter and a tablespoon of treacle.

Potted Shrimps

Serves 1

Time 15 minutes plus chilling
Per portion: 281 Kcal
21g fat (14g saturated)

Unsalted butter 25g (1oz)

Shrimps 75g (3oz), shelled weight

Ground nutmeg small pinch

Ground mace small pinch

Salt and freshly ground black pepper

Brown bread or hot toast to serve

Scan the **QR Code** with a smartphone for an ingredients shopping list

Gently melt the butter in a small saucepan over a very low heat. Simmer gently until a foam rises to the top then remove the foam with a spoon. Carefully pour the clarified butter from the top into a jug and discard the milky residue underneath.

Melt half of the clarified butter and stir in the shrimps, nutmeg, mace and seasoning to taste. Spoon the mixture into a ramekin dish and chill until the mixture has set.

Melt the remaining clarified butter and spoon over the top of the shrimps. Chill once again until the mixture has set.

Serve with toast or crusty brown bread, using the butter layer on top of the ramekins to spread on the toast first.

Cook's TIPS

If you can't find shrimps buy small prawns instead. For special occasions, multiply the quantities by the number of people you are feeding and make the ramekins look pretty with sprigs of dill and a little caviar.

For a delicious alternative to the ubiquitous beans on toast, make one or two little pots of these shrimps and keep in the fridge until you're ready for lunch.

Simple and summery, the crunchy chicken adds delicious texture to this leafy salad, which is served with a tangy tomato dip.

Chicken Goujons with Pea Shoot Salad

 Serves 1

Time 20 minutes
Per portion: 644 Kcal
36g fat (6g saturated)

Mix together the flour, salt and pepper.

Sprinkle the seasoned flour in a shallow dish, the beaten egg in another and the breadcrumbs in another dish.

Toss the chicken strips in the seasoned flour, dip in the beaten egg and then coat evenly in the breadcrumbs, making sure it coats well.

Heat the sunflower oil in a frying pan over a medium heat and fry the chicken on each side for 3-5 minutes, until golden and cooked through. The exact cooking time for the goujons will depend on the thickness of the slices and the temperature of the cooking oil. Remove from the pan, check the chicken is cooked through, and drain on kitchen paper.

Meanwhile, arrange the salad and cucumber on a plate. Mix together the mayonnaise and sun-dried tomato paste. Add the chicken goujons and sun-dried tomato mayonnaise to the plate and enjoy.

Plain flour 1 tbsp

Salt and freshly ground black pepper

Egg 1, beaten

White bread 1-2 slices, crusts removed and blended to make fresh white breadcrumbs

Skinless chicken breast 1 large, sliced into thin strips

Sunflower oil for shallow frying

Pea shoots and baby leaves salad 30g (1oz) (half a packet)

Cucumber 5cm (2in) piece, chopped

Mayonnaise 1–2 tbsp

Sun-dried tomato paste 1 tsp or to taste

 Scan the **QR Code** with a smartphone for an ingredients shopping list

 You can buy small pieces of cucumber in portion sizes in supermarkets.

Use the remaining salad leaves for the recipe on page 25 or mix with Feta cheese and a handful of fresh peas for a delicious salad.

Serves 1

Time 50 minutes
Per portion: 483 Kcal
7g fat (2g saturated)

Southern-Style Chicken with Oven-Baked Chips

Baking potato 1 small, scrubbed and cut into 1cm (½in) thick chips

Sweet potato 1 small, scrubbed and cut into 1cm (½in) thick chips

Olive oil 2 tsp

Hot smoked paprika 1 tsp

Dried onion granules or onion salt 1 tsp

Dried thyme 1 tsp

Plain flour 1 tbsp

Chicken legs 2, skinned

Egg 1, beaten

Dry white breadcrumbs 2-3 tbsp

Tomato ketchup and cooked peas to serve (optional)

 Scan the **QR Code** with a smartphone for an ingredients shopping list

Preheat the oven to 220°C/425°F/Gas 7. Line a large baking sheet with baking parchment. Toss the chips in the oil and then spread out on the sheet.

Mix together ½ teaspoon each of paprika, onion granules or salt and thyme and sprinkle over the potato chips.

Mix the flour with the remaining paprika, onion granules or salt and thyme. Dust the chicken all over with the mixture.

On a plate, beat the egg with 2 tablespoons water, and place the breadcrumbs on another plate. Dip the chicken first in egg and then in crumbs to coat evenly. Place on the prepared baking sheet.

Bake for 30-35 minutes until the chicken is cooked through and the chips are golden.

Serve the chicken and chips with tomato ketchup and peas, if you like.

 Alternatively, serve this diner-style supper with a crisp coleslaw salad tossed in light mayonnaise.

Comfort food with so little effort. This easy chicken and chips recipe is packed full of flavour and healthy too.

No ordinary omelette, this version has a wonderful combination of tangy Cheddar and salty crisp pancetta and is served with a simple pea shoot salad.

Pancetta Omelette with Pea Shoot Salad

 Serves 1

Time 15 minutes
Per portion: 540 Kcal
43g fat (20g saturated)

Fry the pancetta in a non-stick frying pan for 2-3 minutes until crisp. Carefully tip out any excess fat.

Meanwhile, beat together the eggs, pepper, milk and the grated cheese.

Pour the egg and cheese mixture onto the cooked pancetta and swirl around the pan. Cook for 2-3 minutes until the cheese has melted and the omelette is golden underneath and set.

Fold the omelette in half using a palette knife and turn out onto a plate. Quickly arrange the pea shoot salad and cucumber on the plate and serve.

Sliced ready-to-cook pancetta 6–7 rashers, cut into strips
Eggs 2
Freshly ground black pepper
Milk 1 tbsp
Cheddar cheese 50g snack pack portion, grated
Pea shoots and baby leaves salad 30g (1oz), to serve
Cucumber 5cm (2in) piece, chopped, to serve

 Scan the **QR Code** with a smartphone for an ingredients shopping list

 Cook's TIPS

You can buy different sizes of Cheddar cheese portions; a snack pack is 50g per portion but minis are 20g per portion so you will need two.

Pea shoots and baby leaves salads come in small 60g bags, which is the perfect size for two meals for one. Use the remainder with the recipe on page 21.

Use any leftover pancetta in the recipe on page 26.

Pancetta & Mushrooms on Toast with Egg

 Serves 1

Time 10 minutes
Per portion: 152 Kcal
9g fat (3g saturated)

Sliced ready-to-cook pancetta
6–7 rashers, cut into strips

Oyster mushrooms 125g (4½oz), wiped, trimmed and sliced

Freshly ground black pepper

Egg 1

Bread 1 thick slice, toasted

Scan the **QR Code** with a smartphone for an ingredients shopping list

Heat a non-stick frying pan until hot and add the pancetta. Cook for 2-3 minutes until crisp, stirring every now and then.

Add the mushrooms to the pan and fry for about 5 minutes until they start to turn golden. Season with pepper only as the pancetta is already salty.

Meanwhile, bring a small pan of water to a simmer, crack in the egg and poach according to taste.

Pop the hot toast onto a warmed plate and spoon over the hot pancetta and mushroom mix. Top with the poached egg, season with black pepper and serve at once.

Oyster mushrooms come in handy 125g packet sizes; if you would rather use a different mushroom, you will need to weigh the amount you need.

A hearty lunch that only takes minutes to prepare. The salty pancetta contrasts beautifully with the earthy mushrooms and poached egg.

Create your own mildly spiced – or highly spiced if you wish – version of baked beans in this scrumptious ruby-red recipe.

Pan-Fried Pork with Homemade Spicy Beans

 Serves 1

Time 25 minutes
Per portion: 535 Kcal
31g fat (8g saturated)

Heat 2 teaspoons of the oil in a small non-stick pan over a medium heat and cook the onion for about 5 minutes until softened, but not coloured, stirring often. Add the garlic and a pinch of dried chilli flakes and cook for a further minute, stirring.

Add the tomatoes, beans and stock and stir well. Bring to the boil, reduce the heat and cook gently for about 15 minutes, or until the mixture is thickened and reduced, stirring often. Season to taste with salt and pepper.

Meanwhile, heat the remaining teaspoon of oil in a small non-stick pan and cook the pork loin steak for 10–15 minutes, turning once or twice, or until cooked through and no pink colour remains. Leave the pork loin to rest for a few minutes.

Serve the spicy beans on a warmed serving plate and top with the loin steak.

Olive oil 1 tbsp

Onion 1 small, peeled and finely chopped

Garlic 1 clove, peeled and finely chopped

Dried chilli flakes a pinch

Chopped tomatoes 230g can

Butter beans 200g can, rinsed and drained

Hot vegetable stock 150ml (¼ pint)

Salt and freshly ground black pepper

Boneless pork loin steak 1 thick, trimmed of excess fat

 Scan the **QR Code** with a smartphone for an ingredients shopping list

 Cook's TIPS

Small cans of beans and tomatoes are available in supermarkets and are the perfect size for this recipe.

This versatile sauce can be used with grilled sausages or to fill a baked potato; just add a sprinkling of grated cheese for extra protein.

Serves 1

Roast Beef in a Yorkshire Pudding

Time: 10 minutes
Per portion: 409 Kcal
19g fat (6g saturated)

Frozen Yorkshire pudding 1 large

Asparagus tips 3

Reduced fat crème fraîche 1 tbsp

Creamed horseradish sauce 1 tsp

Cooked beetroot 1 large, cut into strips

Watercress a few sprigs

Cooked roast beef 2 slices

Scan the **QR Code** with a smartphone for an ingredients shopping list

Cook the Yorkshire pudding according to the packet's instructions.

Meanwhile, cook the asparagus tips in gently boiling water for 3-4 minutes, until tender. Drain and cut in half lengthways.

Gently mix together the crème fraîche and horseradish sauce. Toss the beetroot, asparagus and watercress in the sauce.

To serve, place the Yorkshire pudding in a bowl and top with slices of beef and the beetroot, asparagus and watercress.

Cook any leftover asparagus, then chop and use to fill an omelette with the leftover watercress and some soft or blue cheese. Serve the omelette with beetroot, if you like.

Yorkshire pudding doesn't have to be served with Sunday dinner – fill it with cooked meat and veg and enjoy it any time as it only takes 10 minutes to prepare.

A super-simple pasta dish that is so quick to prepare. Use your favourite pasta and top with these delicious meatballs in their mildly spiced tomato sauce.

Italian Meatballs

 Serves 1

Time 20 minutes
Per portion: 475 Kcal
10g fat (4g saturated)

Preheat the grill to hot and bring a large saucepan of water to the boil. Add the tagliatelle and cook for 8–10 minutes until tender. At the same time, grill the meatballs for 8–10 minutes, turning several times, until they are evenly browned and cooked through.

Meanwhile, put the onion and spices into a small saucepan with the tomatoes, garlic and a little salt and pepper. Bring to the boil and simmer, uncovered, for 10 minutes, stirring occasionally.

Drain the pasta, add the sauce and toss together. Spoon into a warmed bowl and place the meatballs on top. Sprinkle with basil leaves, if you like.

Tagliatelle 50-75g (2-3oz)
Ready-made meatballs 6
Onion 1 small, peeled and finely chopped
Grated nutmeg ¼ tsp
Ground cinnamon ¼ tsp
Paprika ½ tsp
Chopped tomatoes 230g can
Garlic 1 clove, peeled and crushed
Salt and freshly ground black pepper
Basil leaves to garnish (optional)

Scan the **QR Code** with a smartphone for an ingredients shopping list

If you have any meatballs leftover pop into a freezer bag and freeze ready for next time.

 *Serves 2*

Griddled Halloumi with Wild Rocket

Time 20 minutes
Per portion: 528 Kcal
45g fat (26g saturated)

Halloumi 250g packet, drained
Olive oil 2 tbsp plus 1 tsp
Lime 1, juice only
Garlic 2 cloves, peeled and finely chopped
Freshly ground black pepper
Wild rocket and salad leaves 50g packet, to serve

 Scan the **QR Code** with a smartphone for an ingredients shopping list

Cut the Halloumi into 6–8 thick slices and place in a non-metallic dish.

Mix together the oil, lime juice and garlic, season with plenty of pepper and pour over the Halloumi. Turn the cheese so it is coated in the marinade. Cover and chill for 10 minutes to allow the flavours to infuse.

Oil, then heat a griddle pan over a medium heat. Remove the Halloumi from the marinade, reserving the garlic oil mix, and cook on the hot griddle until golden on both sides. The Halloumi will brown quickly and only needs 1–2 minutes on each side.

Arrange the wild rocket and salad leaves in two bowls and top with Halloumi, drizzle with the reserved garlic oil and serve.

 There is no need to add salt to the dish as Halloumi is already quite salty.

You could also serve with griddled sweet peppers.

Peppery rocket and salad leaves topped with crisp salty Halloumi and a delicious garlicky dressing. A scrumptious lunch for two.

This Moroccan-inspired dish combines fruity, nutty couscous with fresh mint packed inside meltingly soft and sweet roast peppers.

Romano Peppers Stuffed with Fruity Couscous

 *Serves 2*

Time 30 minutes
Per portion: 603 Kcal
36g fat (3g saturated)

Preheat the oven to 220°C/425°F/Gas 7. Put the peppers in a small roasting tin, cut-side down and drizzle with 1 tablespoon of oil. Roast for 10 minutes.

Meanwhile, put the chopped hazelnuts and the pine nuts on a piece of foil on a baking sheet. Put them in the oven above the peppers for 4–5 minutes until toasted.

Meanwhile, put the couscous in a bowl and pour in 100ml (3½fl oz) of boiling water. Stir in the raisins and leave for a few minutes for the water to be absorbed.

Take the peppers out of the oven and turn them over in the roasting tin. Fluff up the couscous and stir in the toasted nuts, capers and most of the torn mint leaves. Season well.

Spoon the couscous mixture into the pepper halves then drizzle with the rest of the oil.

Cover loosely with foil and bake for 8 minutes, then remove the foil and bake for another 5–6 minutes or until browning. Drizzle with more oil and garnish with the remaining mint. Serve hot or cold with salad and a spoonful of harissa yogurt, if you like.

Red Romano peppers 2, cut in half lengthways and deseeded

Olive oil 2 tbsp, plus extra for serving

Blanched hazelnuts 3 tbsp, chopped

Pine nuts 2 tbsp

Couscous 5 tbsp

Raisins 3 tbsp

Capers 1 rounded tbsp, rinsed

Mint leaves 6–10, torn

Salt and freshly ground black pepper

Salad leaves to serve (optional)

Greek yogurt mixed with harissa paste to serve (optional)

 Scan the **QR Code** with a smartphone for an ingredients shopping list

Cook's TIPS

Leave the stalk on the peppers and halve them through the stalk – this makes sure they look good and you also get the deepest receptacle.

Store leftover nuts in an airtight tub and stir a few onto breakfast cereal or into salads.

 Serves 2

Vegetable Chow Mein

Time 15 minutes
Per portion: 328 Kcal
12g fat (2g saturated)

Cornflour 2 tsp
Soy sauce 1 tbsp
Tomato ketchup 1 tbsp
Vegetable stock 150ml (¼ pint)
Root ginger 2cm (¾in) piece, peeled and finely chopped
Garlic 1 clove, peeled and crushed
Olive oil 2 tsp
Mixed vegetable stir-fry 325g pack
Cooked egg noodles 300g pack
Egg 1
Salt and freshly ground black pepper

 Scan the **QR Code** with a smartphone for an ingredients shopping list

Put the cornflour in a small bowl and mix in the soy sauce and ketchup to make a smooth paste. Stir in the stock, ginger and garlic.

Heat 1 teaspoon of the oil in a wok or large frying pan over a medium heat. Add the mixed vegetables and stir-fry for 2 minutes.

Add the noodles to the pan and stir-fry for 1 minute. Mix in the soy mixture and cook for a further 2 minutes until the sauce is boiling and has thickened. Remove from the heat.

Beat the egg with 1 teaspoon of water and a little seasoning. Heat the remaining oil in a small frying pan, pour in the egg and cook, stirring lightly with a fork, until it is browned and set.

Loosen the edges of the omelette and slide it onto a chopping board. Roll it up and cut it into thin slices. Spoon the noodles and vegetables into warmed bowls and top with the omelette strips.

 Stir-fry vegetables are available in many different varieties in the supermarket. Choose the one that contains your favourite mix of vegetables. You can also add beansprouts in to step 3 if you wish.

Who needs a take-away when you have this delicious recipe? The classic combination of crunchy vegetables, tender noodles and egg works perfectly.

Creamy goat's cheese, earthy mushrooms and tangy tomato work beautifully on this crisp pizza. The addition of pesto gives it an extra boost of basil-infused flavour.

Goat's Cheese & Mushroom Pizza

Serves 2

Time 20 minutes
Per portion: 406 Kcal
16g fat (10g saturated)

Preheat the oven to 220°C/425°F/Gas 7.

Set the pizza base onto a baking sheet. Spread the onion relish on the top to make a thin layer, then scatter the tomatoes and mushrooms over the relish. Add the goat's cheese and bake for 10–12 minutes or until the pizza is golden and cooked.

Quickly drizzle the pesto sauce over the top of the pizza, if using. Season to taste and serve topped with a handful of rocket.

Thin and crispy pizza base 1

Onion relish 2–3 tbsp

Tomatoes 2, thinly sliced

Baby mushrooms 50g (2oz), wiped and sliced

Goat's cheese 110g (4oz), sliced and broken into chunks

Green pesto sauce 1 tbsp (optional)

Salt and freshly ground black pepper

Wild rocket about 15g (½oz)

Scan the **QR Code** with a smartphone for an ingredients shopping list

Don't go mad with the onion relish – it is strong but cuts through the richness of the goat's cheese beautifully.

The pesto adds a touch of basil to the tomato, which is lovely, but don't worry if you don't have any to hand as the pizza is tasty without it.

Everyday Eating 41

 Serves 2

Hearty Kiln-Roasted Salmon Salad

Time 20 minutes
Per portion: 346 Kcal
24g fat (4g saturated)

Eggs 2
Fine asparagus tips 100g pack, trimmed
Ready-to-eat mixed grains 250g packet
Wild rocket leaves salad 60g bag
Kiln-roasted Scottish salmon flakes 2 x 100g packets
Lemon 1 small, juice only
Olive oil 3 tbsp
Dijon mustard ½ tsp or to taste
Salt and freshly ground black pepper

 Scan the QR Code with a smartphone for an ingredients shopping list

Put the eggs in a pan of boiling water, cover with a lid, then reduce the heat and simmer for 8–10 minutes until they are hard boiled (a little less if you like them slightly runny in the centre). Drain and run under cold running water for at least a minute. Peel and quarter the eggs and leave them to cool.

Meanwhile, blanch the asparagus in boiling water for a couple of minutes until just tender. Drain and refresh with cold water then drain.

Divide the mixed grains between two plates and top with the wild rocket salad. Arrange the asparagus tips and quartered eggs on top with the kiln-roasted salmon flakes.

Whisk together the lemon juice, oil, mustard and seasoning and pour over the salad. Serve immediately.

 Some supermarkets have slightly larger packets of Scottish roasted salmon flakes (and some are flavoured with honey, which is just as nice), but are usually only 135g packets, so you will still need two.

The mixed grains are sold by Merchant Gourmet in pouches similar to microwave rice.

Filling, full of goodness and absolutely delicious – this salad ticks all the boxes. The combination of flavours and textures works a treat.

This surprising combination of flavours is a taste sensation. It's full of colour and packed with healthy nutrients, such as omega 3 oil.

Baked Salmon Tricolore

 *Serves 2*

Time 30 minutes
Per portion: 726 Kcal
61g fat (11g saturated)

Preheat the oven to 200°C/400°F/Gas 6. Line a baking dish with baking parchment.

Cut the avocado in half and prise out the stone. Peel off the skin and then slice thickly. Arrange in a single layer in the baking dish. Sprinkle with lemon juice. Put the tomatoes in the dish and drizzle with half the oil. Season well.

Mix the mayonnaise with the Parmesan cheese and chopped basil. Lay the fish on top of the avocado and tomatoes and spread the mayonnaise mixture on top of the fish. Then drizzle with the remaining oil.

Bake the salmon in the oven for about 20 minutes, depending on the thickness of the fish, until cooked through and tender. Drain and serve immediately with fresh rocket leaves.

Firm avocado 1 large
Lemon juice 1 tbsp
Tomatoes 2 large, thickly sliced
Olive oil 2 tbsp
Salt and freshly ground black pepper
Garlic mayonnaise 2 tbsp
Grated Parmesan cheese 3 tbsp
Chopped basil 2 tbsp
Salmon fillets 2 x 150g (5oz)
Rocket leaves to serve (optional)

 Scan the **QR Code** with a smartphone for an ingredients shopping list

 Cook's TIPS

Choose a slightly under-ripe avocado for this recipe – it will be easier to peel and slice; the flesh will soften slightly on baking.

If you don't have garlic mayonnaise, mix ordinary mayo with 1 crushed garlic clove.

Everyday Eating 45

 *Serves 2*

Prawn & Mango Curry

Time 30 minutes
Per portion: 683 Kcal
50g fat (32g saturated)

Olive oil 2 tbsp

Spring onions 3, trimmed and sliced

Mangetout 110g (4oz), trimmed

Mango 1 ripe, peeled, stoned and thinly sliced

Medium curry paste 2 tbsp

Coconut cream 200ml carton

Cooked king prawns 200g (7oz)

Chopped coriander 4 tbsp, plus sprigs to garnish

Cooked basmati rice to serve

 Scan the **QR Code** with a smartphone for an ingredients shopping list

Heat the olive oil in a large wok, add the spring onions and mangetout and stir-fry for about 5 minutes until both are softened, yet still retain a slight crispness.

Add the mango and curry paste and continue cooking for 1–2 minutes. Pour the coconut cream into the wok, then add the prawns and heat through until the mixture is piping hot, but not boiling.

Stir in the chopped coriander and serve in warmed bowls garnished with the coriander sprigs and accompanied with cooked basmati rice.

 Stir-fry any leftover mangetout and spring onions until softened and mix with egg-fried rice.

This creamy coconut-infused curry combines succulent king prawns with crisp mangetout and sweet, soft mango for a decadent mix of flavours and textures.

A welcome change from a standard burger, these chicken pieces are infused with a fiery lemon glaze, which contrasts with the rustic bread and salad beautifully.

Spiced Chicken on a Bun

 Serves 2

Time 30 minutes
Per portion: 613 Kcal
28g fat (4g saturated)

Put the chicken breasts, skinned-side down, on a large piece of cling film and slash them a couple of times so they can be opened out. Put another piece of cling film on top, then bash the meat with a rolling pin until it is about 1cm (about ½in) thick all over.

In a small bowl, mix together the lemon juice, oil, harissa paste and salt.

Brush the harissa mix liberally over the chicken, discarding any leftover harissa mix.

Preheat a griddle over a medium heat and cook the chicken for 7 minutes on each side, or until the juices run clear.

Meanwhile, cut each roll in half and spread with mayonnaise. Fill with lettuce, tomato slices, chicken and red onion. Serve straight away.

Skinless chicken breasts 2
Lemon 1 small, juice only
Olive oil 1–2 tbsp
Harissa paste 1 tsp
Salt
Rustic rolls 2
Mayonnaise 1–2 tbsp
Little Gem lettuce 1, trimmed, washed and sliced
Tomato 1 large, sliced
Red onion 1 small, peeled and finely sliced

 Scan the **QR Code** with a smartphone for an ingredients shopping list

 Harissa paste, once opened, should be stored in the fridge. To use up any that is leftover, stir a little paste into couscous or Greek yogurt and chopped mint for a spicy Moroccan-style side dish.

 *Serves 2*

Thai Chicken Skewers

Time 25 minutes
Per portion: 500 Kcal
16g fat (6g saturated)

Thai red or green curry paste 1 tbsp

Coconut cream 2 tbsp

Skinless chicken breasts 2, cut into 2cm (¾in) squares

Mixed red and white quinoa with bulgur wheat 150g (5oz)

Hot chicken or vegetable stock 300ml (½ pint)

Peeled and finely grated root ginger 2 tsp

Spring onions 2, trimmed and finely chopped

Sesame oil 2 tsp

Chopped coriander 4 tbsp

Lime wedges 2

 Scan the **QR Code** with a smartphone for an ingredients shopping list

Mix the curry paste and coconut cream in a shallow bowl. Add the chicken and leave for 10 minutes. Soak 6 bamboo skewers in cold water.

Meanwhile, put the quinoa mix and hot stock into a pan and bring to the boil. Reduce the heat, cover and simmer for 12 minutes or until the stock has been absorbed.

Take the pan off the heat, stir in the ginger, spring onions and sesame oil and then the coriander.

While the quinoa is cooking, heat a griddle pan or the grill and thread the chicken onto the skewers. Griddle or grill for 3–5 minutes on each side until the chicken is cooked through.

Serve the quinoa on warmed plates together with the skewers and the lime wedges.

 Use any leftover coconut cream to make a Thai curry, with Thai paste, chopped spring onions and prawns.

Quinoa can be used as an alternative to couscous, rice or bulgur wheat. Add it to salads for a bit of extra substance.

Delicious Thai chicken skewers served on a bed of ginger-spiced nutty quinoa and bulgur wheat mixed with coriander.

The mustard mayo served with these thyme-flavoured chicken escalopes works wonderfully well, and the green vegetables add colour and freshness to the dish.

Chicken Escalopes with Thyme and Courgette

Serves 2

Time 25 minutes
Per portion: 359 Kcal
23g fat (4g saturated)

Put the chicken breasts, skinned-side down, on a large piece of cling film and slash them a couple of times so they can be opened out. Put another piece of cling film on top, then bash the meat with a rolling pin until it is about 1cm (about ½in) thick all over.

Take off the top layer of cling film and rub half the oil all over the chicken. Season well and scatter with thyme leaves.

Heat a griddle pan over a high heat. Put the chicken onto the griddle and cook for 2–3 minutes on each side, pressing it down to get good griddle marks.

Meanwhile, rub the rest of the oil onto the courgette slices and spring onions. When the chicken is cooked, transfer it to warmed plates, loosely cover them and keep warm in the oven. Put the courgette slices and spring onions onto the griddle and cook for 3–4 minutes each side.

While the courgettes and spring onions are cooking, mix the mayonnaise and mustard together in a bowl and season to taste.

Serve the chicken with the courgettes and spring onions and a sprinkling of chopped thyme together with the sauce and new potatoes, if you like.

Skinless chicken breasts 2
Olive oil 1 tbsp
Salt and freshly ground black pepper
Chopped thyme 1 heaped tsp, plus extra to serve
Courgette 1, trimmed and cut into 6 long thin slices
Spring onions 4–6, trimmed to about 8cm (3in) lengths
Mayonnaise 4 heaped tsp
English mustard 1 tsp
Steamed new potatoes to serve (optional)

Scan the **QR Code** with a smartphone for an ingredients shopping list

Bashing out chicken breasts means you can cook them very quickly. While you're bashing, do a few more and freeze them individually. They don't take long to thaw for quick suppers.

 *Serves 2*

Stir-Fried Pork with Egg-Fried Rice

Time 15 minutes
Per portion: 674 Kcal
34g fat (11g saturated)

Long grain rice 110g (4oz)

Sunflower oil 4 tsp

Boneless pork loin chop 225g (8oz), fat removed and meat cut into thin crossways slices

Carrots 2, peeled and thinly sliced

Green cabbage 110g (4oz), cored and finely shredded

Garlic 1 clove, peeled and crushed

Tomato ketchup 2 tbsp

Soy sauce 2 tbsp

Sherry or stock 2 tbsp

Ground ginger ¼ tsp

Spring onions 2, trimmed and thinly sliced

Egg 1, beaten

 Scan the **QR Code** with a smartphone for an ingredients shopping list

Cook the rice in a saucepan of boiling water for 10 minutes until just tender.

Meanwhile, heat 3 teaspoons of the oil in a wok or large non-stick frying pan. Add the pork and carrots and stir-fry for 7 minutes.

Add the cabbage and garlic and stir-fry for a further 5 minutes.

Add the ketchup, soy sauce, sherry or stock and ginger and mix them together.

Drain the rice, then rinse it in hot water and drain again. Dry the saucepan and in it heat the remaining teaspoon of oil. Add the spring onions and cook for 1 minute, then add the rice and beaten egg and cook, stirring until the egg looks scrambled.

Spoon the rice and pork stir-fry into warmed bowls and serve immediately.

 Cook any leftover spring onions with vegetable stock and then whizz in a blender with soft cheese to make a tasty soup. Shred any remaining cabbage and mix with grated carrot, chopped nuts, raisins and mayonnaise to make a fruity crunchy salad.

A rich, colourful, and very tasty pork stir-fry, which is served with classic fluffy egg-fried rice.

Perfect for a blustery day, this comforting combination of creamy mash and rosemary lamb with a hint of chilli is just what's required to warm you up.

Spicy Lamb with Creamy Mash

 Serves 2

Time 30 minutes
Per portion: 629 Kcal
38g fat (15g saturated)

Put the potatoes in a pan with just enough water to cover them. Bring to the boil, cover with the lid, then reduce the heat and simmer for 18–20 minutes until they are tender.

Drain the potatoes, return them to the pan and place it over a low heat for a few seconds to remove any moisture. Mash, then beat in the butter and warmed milk, a little at a time, until the potatoes are soft and silky. Season to taste.

Meanwhile, set the lamb chops or steaks on a plate. Mix together the oil, chilli flakes, garlic and rosemary and brush the mixture liberally over both sides of the lamb steaks.

Heat a non-stick frying pan over a medium heat with any leftover oil mix. Add the lamb steaks and cook for 2–3 minutes on each side; the exact time depends on the thickness of the steak and how well you like your lamb cooked.

Remove the lamb from the pan. Season to taste with salt and leave to rest for a couple of minutes.

Spoon a pile of mash onto warmed plates and flatten slightly, spoon the lamb on top and serve with vegetables cooked in the microwave according to the packet's instructions.

Maris Piper or King Edward potatoes 450g (1lb), peeled and cut into even-sized chunks

Butter 15g (½oz)

Milk 75ml (3fl oz), warmed

Salt and freshly ground black pepper

Lean lamb rump chops or lamb leg steaks 2

Olive oil 2 tbsp

Dried chilli flakes a pinch

Garlic 2 cloves, peeled and chopped

Dried rosemary a pinch

Steamed vegetables such as a 285g packet of minted green vegetables, including beans, peas and cabbage

 Scan the **QR Code** with a smartphone for an ingredients shopping list

 Cook's TIPS

If you are short of time you can always buy a tub of ready-made mash and heat according to the packet's instructions.

If you can only buy leg steaks, you will need to increase the cooking time on both sides.

 *Serves 2*

Cheat's Beef Curry

Time 10 minutes
Per portion: 256 Kcal
13g fat (3g saturated)

Vegetable oil 1 tbsp

Beef steak strips 225g (8oz)

Chopped tomatoes 400g can

Medium curry paste 2 tbsp

Microwave pilau rice 250g packet

Fried onion slices to garnish (optional)

Torn coriander leaves to garnish (optional)

Naan bread to serve (optional)

Scan the **QR Code** with a smartphone for an ingredients shopping list

Heat the oil in a large frying pan over a medium heat and fry the beef for 2–3 minutes or until browned.

Add the tomatoes and curry paste, bring to the boil and simmer for 3–4 minutes.

Meanwhile, heat the rice according to the packet's instructions. Serve the curry on a bed of rice garnished with onion slices and coriander, if using, and warm naan bread, if you like.

You could also add a handful of frozen peas or sweetcorn, if you like. Just simmer for a little longer.

Who would have thought that a homemade curry could be this quick? Throw together a few ingredients and this sumptuous beef curry can be on the table in 10 minutes!

Eat & Freeze

Four Veg & Ricotta Cannelloni	62
Broccoli & Stilton Quiches	65
Golden-Topped Fish Pies	66
Thai Fishcakes with Crunchy Salad	69
Chicken Casserole with Thyme & Orange	70
Chicken with Mushrooms & Tarragon	73
Pork & Pumpkin Casserole	74
Cheesy Bacon Mash	77
Sausage & Artichoke Rolls	78
Spinach Sausages with Garlicky Tomato Sauce	81
Braised Lamb with Lemon & Parsnips	82
Moroccan Mince	85
Beef Goulash	86
Warming Beef in Beer Stew	89
Cornish Pasties	90
Beef & Polenta Pies	93
Apple & Mint Sorbet	94
Lemon Swirl Biscuits	97
Anzac Biscuits	98
Fruit Slices	101
No-Bake Chocolate Squares	102
Blueberry & Buttermilk Muffins	105
Buttermilk & Cinnamon Scones	106
Ginger & Prune Scones	109
Sticky Walnut Tart	110
Raspberry Swiss Roll	113
Banana & Sultana Loaf	114
Cornish Saffron Cake	117
Chocolate Fudgey Cake	118

Four Veg & Ricotta Cannelloni

Makes 6 individual dishes

Time 1½ hours
Per portion: 339 Kcal
18g fat (9g saturated)

Olive oil 1 tbsp

Garlic 2 cloves, peeled and finely chopped

Butternut squash ½ (about 350g/12oz peeled and deseeded weight), coarsely grated

Carrot 1 large, peeled and coarsely grated

Courgette 1 large, trimmed and coarsely grated

Spinach leaves 150g (5oz)

Salt and freshly ground black pepper

Dried lasagne sheets 12

Eggs 2

Ricotta cheese 500g (1lb 2oz)

Chopped tomatoes 2 x 400g cans

Grated Mozzarella cheese 110g (4oz)

Scan the QR Code with a smartphone for an ingredients shopping list

Heat the oil in a large frying pan and fry the garlic for 1 minute. Add the squash, carrot and courgette and cook, stirring, for about 4 minutes until just softened. Stir in the spinach and season generously with salt and pepper.

Add 3 lasagne sheets at a time to a pan of boiling water and boil for 3 minutes. Remove with tongs and put them straight into a bowl of cold water.

Beat the eggs in a large bowl, add the Ricotta and beat until almost smooth. Add half of this to the cooked vegetables and mix well.

Lay all the lasagne sheets out on two tea towels, cut them in half to make 24 almost square pieces and divide the Ricotta/veg mixture between them.

Roll up each piece of pasta and place, join-side down, in six gratin dishes, using four per dish. Spoon the tomatoes over and season. Spoon the remaining Ricotta mixture on top and sprinkle with Mozzarella.

To serve now: Preheat the oven to 180°C/350°F/Gas 4. Cover the dishes with foil and bake for 30 minutes. Remove the foil, increase the oven to 200°C/400°F/Gas 6 and bake for another 15–20 minutes until browned and bubbling. Leave for 5–10 minutes before serving.

To freeze: Cover the dishes with foil, put into a polybag, seal, label and freeze. Use within 3 months.

To serve from the freezer: Take the dishes out of the polybags and thaw in the fridge overnight. Cook as above.

Comfort food at its best – these homemade ready meals are perfect for popping in the oven when you fancy a veggie pasta feast.

Broccoli and cheese provide the perfect combination of flavours for a quiche. These mini quiches are ideal for making ahead so that you can enjoy a real midweek treat.

Broccoli & Stilton Quiches

Makes 4 quiches

Time 1 hour
Per quiche: 303 Kcal
Fat 20g (9g saturated)

Roll out the pastry and use to line four 10cm (4in) diameter flan tins.

Melt the butter in a saucepan, add the onion and cook gently for 3–4 minutes until softened.

Blanch the broccoli in boiling water for 2–3 minutes. Pour into a sieve, rinse under cold water and drain.

Divide the onion, broccoli and Stilton between the four tins.

To serve now: Preheat the oven to 220°C /425°F/ Gas 7. Mix together 1 egg and 100ml (3½fl oz) milk. Pour into two tins, season and mix gently. Place on a baking tray. Bake for 20–30 minutes until set and golden. Allow to cool slightly before removing from the tins. Serve warm.

To freeze: Wrap the assembled quiches in cling film and pack into a plastic container. Seal, label and use within 4 months.

To serve from the freezer: Unwrap two tins, and cook as above (adding egg and milk); there's no need to defrost.

Shortcrust pastry 150g (5oz)
Butter 15g (½oz)
Onion 1 small, peeled and chopped
Small broccoli florets 75g (3oz)
Stilton 50g (2oz), crumbled
When ready to cook: serves 2
Egg 1
Milk 100ml (3½fl oz)
Salt and freshly ground black pepper

Scan the **QR Code** with a smartphone for an ingredients shopping list

These can be cooked straight from the freezer, which is perfect for when you're short of time. Simply add with the egg and milk before baking.

If you have any egg and milk mixture left, mix with 1–2 tsp sugar and orange zest, pour into a ramekin and bake with the quiches for a scrumptious baked custard.

If you don't have individual flan tins you could use metal poachette rings set on a baking tray.

Eat & Freeze 65

Makes 4 individual pies

Golden-Topped Fish Pies

Time 1¼ hours
Per portion: 441 Kcal
16g fat (8g saturated)

Sweet potatoes about 350g (12oz), peeled and cut into even-sized chunks

Potatoes 350g (12oz), peeled and cut into even-sized chunks

Milk 4 tbsp, plus 600ml (1 pint)

Butter 65g (2½oz)

Fish pie mix of fish about 450g (1lb) from the fish counter, to include salmon, white fish and smoked haddock

Leek 1, trimmed, washed and sliced

Plain flour 50g (2oz)

Chopped parsley 4–5 tbsp

Salt and freshly ground black pepper

Scan the **QR Code** with a smartphone for an ingredients shopping list

Put all the potatoes in a large pan with just enough water to cover. Bring to the boil, cover, then simmer for 18–20 minutes until tender.

Drain the potatoes, return to the pan and place it over a low heat to remove any moisture. Mash with the 4 tablespoons of milk and 15g (½oz) of butter.

Meanwhile, put the fish mix into a pan with 600ml (1 pint) milk. Bring just to the boil, then take off the heat and cover with a lid. Leave for 5 minutes. Drain the fish, reserving the milk, and clean the pan.

Melt 25g butter in the pan over a medium heat. Stir in the leek, cover and simmer for 7 minutes, stirring occasionally. Divide the leek and fish between four 250ml (8fl oz) ovenproof or foil dishes.

Melt 25g butter in the pan, add the flour and cook over a medium heat for 1–2 minutes. Gradually beat in the reserved milk and whisk to make a sauce. Cook for 2 minutes, then add the parsley and season.

Spoon the sauce into the dishes and top with spoonfuls of mash.

To serve now: Preheat the oven to 200°C/400°F/Gas 6. Put one or two of the fish pies on a baking sheet in the oven and bake for 35–40 minutes or until the filling is bubbling hot.

To freeze: Cover the uncooked dishes with foil. Seal, label and freeze. Use within 2 months.

To serve from the freezer: Remove from the freezer and thaw in the fridge overnight. Cook as above.

These little pots of loveliness give a modern twist to traditional fish pie with a creamy orange-hued sweet potato topping.

Wow! Make your own scrumptious salmon fish cakes packed full of Thai flavours and accompanied by a sweet and simple crunchy salad.

Thai Fishcakes with Crunchy Salad

Makes 4 fishcakes

Time 15 minutes
Per fishcake: 153 Kcal
10g fat (2g saturated)

To make the fishcakes, put the salmon, curry paste, ginger, fish or soy sauce and coriander in a bowl and mash together with a potato masher or stick blender.

Shape into four cakes about 1.5cm (¾in) thick and 6–7cm (2½–2¾in) in diameter.

To serve now: Heat a non-stick frying pan over a medium heat and spray the fish cakes with a little oil. Fry two per person for 2 minutes on each side until they are crisp and golden. Serve with sweet chilli sauce, if using, and salad (see next step).

To make the salad, use a swivel headed peeler to ribbon the carrot, cucumber and courgette into a salad bowl. Mix together the lime juice, fish sauce, oil and sugar, then toss into the salad with the herbs.

To freeze: Wrap each uncooked fishcake in non-stick parchment and pack in a polybag. Seal, label and freeze. Use within 1 month.

To serve from the freezer: Take fishcakes out of their packaging and thaw in the fridge for 2 hours or a few minutes in the microwave on defrost. Cook as above and serve with salad.

Skinless salmon fillets 2, chopped
Thai red curry paste 1 tbsp
Peeled and finely grated root ginger 1–2 tsp
Thai fish sauce or soy sauce 1 tsp
Chopped coriander 3 tbsp
Spray cooking oil

For the salad: serves 2
Carrot 1 small, peeled
Cucumber about ¼
Courgette 1 small, trimmed
Lime juice 1 tsp
Thai fish sauce 1 tsp
Sesame oil 2 tsp
Sugar a pinch
Mint and coriander leaves a small handful of each
Sweet chilli dipping sauce (optional)

Scan the **QR Code** with a smartphone for an ingredients shopping list

Four fishcakes will serve 2 people. Double up the quantity if you want to serve 2 and freeze extras.

For a more substantial meal, serve with medium egg noodles (1 nest between two people) or Thai Jasmine rice.

Use white fish if you prefer. If you're not keen on Thai, just mix the fish with lemon zest, nutmeg and seasoning.

If you don't have spray oil use 2 tsp olive oil instead.

Chicken Casserole with Thyme & Orange

Makes 4 individual portions

Time 1½ hours
Per portion: 488 Kcal
33g fat (9g saturated)

Sunflower oil 2 tsp
Chicken thighs 4
Chicken drumsticks 4
Onion 1 large, peeled and finely chopped
Plain flour 1 tbsp
Chicken stock 300ml (½ pint)
Orange 1, grated zest and juice
Thyme few sprigs or ½ tsp dried
Salt and freshly ground black pepper
Mash and baby carrots to serve (optional)

Scan the QR Code with a smartphone for an ingredients shopping list

Preheat the oven to 180°C/350°F/Gas 4.

Heat the oil in a frying pan over a medium heat. Add the chicken pieces and onion and fry for about 8 minutes until lightly browned.

Stir in the flour and add the stock, orange zest and juice, thyme and a little salt and pepper. Spoon into a casserole dish, cover and cook in the oven for 1 hour.

To serve now: Spoon portions onto warmed plates, and serve with mash and baby carrots, if you like.

To freeze: Allow the casserole to cool completely. Spoon portions into small polybags. Seal, label and freeze. Use within 4 months.

To serve from the freezer: Take out as many portions as required and put the bags into a dish. Defrost overnight in the fridge. Pour into a saucepan, cover and reheat, stirring, until piping hot.

 You could use a lemon instead of the orange, and if you prefer, you can use chicken breasts.

70 Eat & Freeze

One pot cooking at its best, this combination of tangy orange with fragrant thyme works its magic with the chicken.

This is a classic for a reason – it tastes superb! The subtle aniseed flavour of the tarragon gives an edge to the sauce, which works perfectly with the chicken and mushrooms.

Chicken with Mushrooms & Tarragon

Makes 4 individual portions

Time 55 minutes
Per portion: 603 Kcal
48g fat (24g saturated)

Heat half the oil in a large saucepan or frying pan and cook the shallots, garlic and mushrooms for 5 minutes or until softened. Remove from the pan with a slotted spoon. Add the chicken breasts to the pan with the remaining oil and cook for about 10 minutes, or until golden on both sides.

Add the wine to the pan and bring to the boil, then reduce the heat and simmer for 5–10 minutes, or until reduced by half. Add the cream with the reserved mushroom mixture and tarragon and bring to the boil, then reduce the heat and simmer for 15–20 minutes, or until the chicken is cooked through and the creamy sauce is thickened and reduced. Stir every now and then.

To serve now: Season to taste and spoon onto warmed plates. Serve with green beans if you like.

To freeze: Allow to cool completely. Spoon portions into small polybags. Seal, label and freeze. Use within 4 months.

To serve from the freezer: Take out as many portions as required and put the bags into a dish. Defrost overnight in the fridge. Pour into a saucepan, cover and reheat gently, stirring, until piping hot.

Olive oil 2 tbsp

Shallots 2, peeled, halved and thinly sliced

Garlic 1–2 cloves, peeled and crushed

Shiitake mushrooms 120g punnet, wiped and sliced

Closed cup mushrooms 250g punnet, wiped and sliced

Skinless chicken breasts 4

White wine 150ml (¼ pint)

Double cream 300ml (½ pint)

Chopped tarragon 2 tbsp, plus extra for garnish

Salt and freshly ground black pepper

Green beans to serve (optional)

Scan the **QR Code** with a smartphone for an ingredients shopping list

Cook's TIPS

If you can't find, or don't like the shiitake mushrooms, then use the same quantity of oyster or field mushrooms.

This is delicious served with garlic bread.

Pork & Pumpkin Casserole

Makes 4 individual portions

Time 2 hours
Per portion: 358 Kcal
27g fat (9g saturated)

Olive oil 2 tbsp
Boneless pork shoulder steaks 4
Onion 1, peeled and chopped
Ground ginger 1 tsp
Ground cinnamon 1 tsp
Ground turmeric 1 tsp
Plain flour 1 tbsp
Pumpkin 400g (14oz), peeled, deseeded and cut into chunks
Chicken stock 600ml (1 pint)
Light muscovado sugar 1 tbsp
Salt and freshly ground black pepper
Mashed potatoes and peas to serve (optional)

Scan the **QR Code** with a smartphone for an ingredients shopping list

Preheat the oven to 180°C/350°F/Gas 4. Heat the oil in a large frying pan over a medium heat and fry the pork for about 8 minutes until browned on both sides. Drain and transfer to a large casserole dish.

Fry the onion in the pan juices for about 5 minutes until softened.

Stir the spices and flour into the onion. Add the pumpkin, stock, sugar, salt and pepper, bring to the boil and then pour over the pork.

Cover the casserole dish with a lid and cook in the oven for about 1½ hours until the pork is tender.

To serve now: Spoon the casserole onto warmed plates and serve with mashed potatoes and peas.

To freeze: Allow the casserole to cool completely, then transfer portions into small polybags. Seal, label and freeze. Use within 3 months.

To serve from the freezer: Take out as many portions as required, put into an ovenproof dish and defrost in the fridge overnight. Remove the bags, cover the dish with foil and cook at 190°C/375°F/Gas 5 for 30 minutes until piping hot.

If pumpkin isn't available, use butternut squash instead. You could also serve this dish with rice or couscous.

Spiced soft, sweet pumpkin with tender pork that just falls apart on your plate – this is what slow cooking is all about.

Speedy and versatile, this delicious mash can be warmed through in minutes and served with whatever takes your fancy!

Cheesy Bacon Mash

Makes 4 individual portions

Time 40 minutes
Per portion: 329 Kcal
18g fat (9g saturated)

Put the potatoes in a large pan with just enough water to cover. Bring to the boil, cover with the lid, then reduce the heat and simmer for 18–20 minutes until tender.

Drain the potatoes, return them to the pan and place it over a low heat to remove any moisture. Mash, then beat in the milk and butter, a little at a time, until the potato is soft and silky.

Meanwhile dry-fry the rashers of bacon in a non-stick pan. When really crispy, drain on kitchen paper.

Snip the bacon rashers into the mash and add the spring onions along with most of the cheese. Season well and remove the pan from the heat.

Divide the mixture between 4 ovenproof and freezerproof dishes and sprinkle with the remaining Cheddar cheese.

To serve now: Preheat the grill to medium and put each dish under the grill to brown the cheese. Serve the mash with a poached or fried egg on top if you like, or with sausages, beans, pork chop or chicken.

To freeze: Cover the dishes with cling film. Label and freeze. Use within 2 months.

To serve from the freezer: Remove the dish from the freezer and thaw in the fridge overnight. Cook as above, ensuring that it's piping hot.

Potatoes 700g (1½lb), peeled and cut into even-sized chunks

Milk 100ml (3½fl oz)

Butter 15g (½oz)

Streaky bacon rashers 4

Spring onions 4, trimmed and finely chopped

Cheddar cheese 75g (3oz), grated

Salt and freshly ground black pepper

Poached or fried egg to serve (optional)

Sausages, baked beans, pork chop or chicken to serve (optional)

Scan the **QR Code** with a smartphone for an ingredients shopping list

The mixture could be frozen in plastic tubs then, when thawed, fried to reheat and made into a hash, adding leftover cooked greens and topped with a fried egg.

Sausage & Artichoke Rolls

Makes 4 individual portions

Time 1½ hours
Per portion: 661 Kcal
46g fat (19g saturated)

Lincolnshire or Cumberland sausages 8 (approx. 500g/1lb 2oz)

Spring onions 4, trimmed and chopped

Salt and freshly ground black pepper

Chilled ready-rolled puff pastry 375g pack

English mustard 2 heaped tsp

Chargrilled artichoke 6 pieces

Beaten egg for glazing

Scan the **QR Code** with a smartphone for an ingredients shopping list

Skin the sausages and mix the meat in a bowl with the spring onions and lots of seasoning. Line two baking sheets with non-stick parchment paper.

Unroll and cut the pastry into four pieces. Roll out two pieces a little more, each to a rectangle 19 x 12cm (7½ x 5in) and transfer to the baking sheets.

Spread 1 teaspoon of the mustard over each piece of pastry, leaving a 2.5cm (1in) border. Divide the meat into four and spread one of the portions along each of the pastry bases. Lay three of the artichoke pieces on top of each portion and then top with the remaining meat. Brush the pastry edge with water.

Roll out the remaining pastry a little larger than the first, about 20 x 14cm (8 x 5½in). Lay them carefully over the top of the meat and seal well around the filling. Trim the edges. Each slice will serve 2.

To serve now: Chill the slice while the oven heats up to 200°C/400°F/Gas 6. Brush a little egg over the pastry and score the top a few times. Bake for 50–55 minutes in the lower half of the oven to ensure the pastry base is crisp and eat while still hot.

To freeze: Open-freeze the remaining slice on the baking sheet until solid, then take the slice off the baking sheet and put it in a polybag. Seal, label and freeze. Use within 2 months.

To serve from the freezer: Take the slice out of its bag, keeping it on the paper, and thaw in the fridge overnight. Cook as above.

This surprising combination of ingredients is a taste sensation that turns an everyday sausage roll into a delicious golden parcel of contrasting flavours.

A delicious alternative to bangers and mash, serve these scrumptious pork and spinach sausages with the vibrant tomato sauce.

Spinach Sausages with Garlicky Tomato Sauce

Makes 4 individual portions

Time 1 hour plus chilling
Per portion: 443 Kcal
32g fat (11g saturated)

Put the spinach into a sieve and press out the water with a spoon. Line a baking sheet with foil.

Put half the onions into a bowl with the spinach, sausage meat, breadcrumbs, cinnamon and plenty of salt and pepper. Mix together. With wet hands shape the mixture into 12 small sausages. Place on the baking sheet and chill for 30 minutes.

To make the sauce, heat the oil in a frying pan and cook the remaining onion for 5 minutes until soft. Add the garlic, sugar and tomatoes and season to taste. Bring to the boil, then simmer for 10 minutes.

To serve now: Heat the grill to hot. Cook three sausages per person under the grill for 15 minutes, turning occasionally, until they are evenly browned and cooked through. Serve on a bed of rice with the sauce spooned over the top.

To freeze: Allow the sauce to cool completely and then pack portions into small polybags. Open-freeze the raw sausages on a baking tray and then wrap in cling film and store in a plastic tub. Seal, label and freeze. Use with 4 months.

To serve from the freezer: Take out as many portions as required and put into a saucepan, still in their bags. Defrost overnight in the fridge. Remove the bags, heat the sauce through in the saucepan and grill the sausages as above.

Frozen leaf spinach 110g (4oz), defrosted

Onions 2, peeled and finely chopped

Pork sausage meat 450g (1lb)

White breadcrumbs 50g (2oz)

Ground cinnamon ½ tsp

Salt and freshly ground black pepper

Olive oil 1 tbsp

Garlic 1 clove, peeled and crushed

Sugar 1 tsp

Chopped tomatoes 400g can

Cooked rice to serve (optional)

Scan the **QR Code** with a smartphone for an ingredients shopping list

As an alternative to rice, you could serve the sausages in warm pitta bread, topped with the tomato sauce.

Braised Lamb with Lemon & Parsnips

Makes 4 individual portions

Time 2¼ hours
Per portion: 514 Kcal
32g fat (13g saturated)

Olive oil 2 tbsp
Diced lamb 600g (1lb 5oz)
Onions 2, peeled and chopped
Parsnips 450g (1lb), peeled and chopped
Plain flour 1 tbsp
Lamb stock 600ml (1 pint)
Salt and freshly ground black pepper
Lemon 1 large, sliced and pips removed
Chopped sage 1 tbsp fresh or 2 tsp dried
Rice and steamed runner beans to serve (optional)

Scan the **QR Code** with a smartphone for an ingredients shopping list

Preheat the oven to 180°C/350°F/Gas 4. Heat the oil in a large saucepan or frying pan and fry the lamb for about 10 minutes until it is browned on all sides. Remove the meat from the pan with a slotted spoon and transfer it to a large casserole dish or deep roasting tin.

Fry the onions in the pan juices for about 5 minutes until softened. Add the parsnips and fry for 2 minutes, stirring.

Stir in the flour and then add the stock, seasoning, lemon slices and sage. Bring to the boil, then transfer to the casserole dish.

Cover and cook in the oven for 1¾ hours until the lamb is tender.

To serve now: Spoon into warmed bowls and serve with rice and steamed runner beans if liked.

To freeze: Allow to cool completely. Spoon into polybags. Seal, label and freeze. Use within 4 months.

To serve from the freezer: Take out as many portions as required and put into a dish, still in their bags. Defrost overnight in the fridge. Then pour into a saucepan, cover and bring slowly to the boil. Continue to cook, stirring, until piping hot.

Ready-diced lamb usually comes in 300g packs and is often included in promotional offers. Buying and cooking in bulk can save pounds and provide you with plenty of delicious ready meals.

The meltingly tender lamb, velvety soft parsnips and piquant lemon make a surprising but scrumptious combination.

If you're after comfort food, look no further. This Moroccan-inspired minced beef dish is packed full of sweet spices, vegetables and pulses.

Moroccan Mince

Makes 4 individual portions

Time 2 hours
Per portion: 284 Kcal
10g fat (4g saturated)

Preheat the oven to 180°C/350°F/Gas 4. Heat the oil in a large saucepan or wok and fry the onion with the mince, stirring for 5-8 minutes, until the mince is evenly browned.

Add the carrots and parsnips to the mince with the garlic and fry for 2–3 minutes, stirring. Then stir in the lentils, chickpeas, tomatoes, tomato purée, spices and stock.

Finally, stir the raisins into the mince and season to taste. Bring to the boil and transfer to a large casserole dish. Cover and cook in the oven for 1¼ hours.

To serve now: Spoon portions into warmed bowls and serve with couscous if liked.

To freeze: Allow to cool completely. Spoon into polybags. Seal, label and freeze. Use within 4 months.

To serve from the freezer: Take out as many portions as required and put into a bowl, still in their bags. Defrost overnight in the fridge. Then pour into a saucepan, cover and bring slowly to the boil (you may need to add a little boiling water). Continue to cook, stirring, until piping hot.

Olive oil 1 tbsp

Onion 1 small, peeled and chopped

Minced beef or lamb 250g (9oz)

Carrots 110g (4oz), peeled and diced

Parsnips 110g (4oz), peeled and diced

Garlic 1 clove, peeled and crushed

Green lentils 50g (2oz), rinsed and drained

Chickpeas 210g can, drained

Chopped tomatoes 200g can

Tomato purée 1 tbsp

Ground turmeric ½ tsp

Ground ginger 1 tsp

Ground cinnamon 1 tsp

Ground coriander 2 tsp

Chicken stock 450ml (¾ pint)

Raisins 50g (2oz)

Salt and freshly ground black pepper

Couscous to serve (optional)

Scan the **QR Code** with a smartphone for an ingredients shopping list

This recipe is great value for money as just 250g (9oz) mince provides four hearty portions. Any root vegetable works well in this dish.

Eat & Freeze 85

Makes 4 individual portions

Beef Goulash

Time 3–3½ hours
Per portion: 449 Kcal
22g fat (9g saturated)

Sunflower oil 3 tbsp
Onions 2, peeled and chopped
Garlic 2 cloves, peeled and finely chopped
Red pepper 1 small, deseeded and thinly sliced
Green pepper 1 small, deseeded and thinly sliced
Lean braising steak 2 x 400g packets
Plain flour 2 tbsp
Hot smoked paprika 1 tsp
Chopped tomatoes 2 x 400g cans
Beef stock 150ml (¼ pint)
Salt and freshly ground black pepper
Soured cream to serve (optional)
Boiled rice to serve (optional)

Scan the **QR Code** with a smartphone for an ingredients shopping list

Preheat the oven to 160°C/325°F/Gas 3. Heat half the oil in a large frying pan and cook the onions for about 5 minutes until softened, stirring often.

Add the garlic and cook for about 2 minutes. Spoon the onions and garlic into a casserole dish.

Cook the peppers in the pan for about 5 minutes until softened, then remove to the casserole dish.

Toss the steak in the flour and cook in batches for about 10 minutes until the meat is browned, adding the remaining oil as necessary.

Add the paprika, tomatoes, stock and seasoning. Slowly bring to the boil, stirring all the time.

Transfer to the casserole dish, mix well, cover and bake for 2–2½ hours until the meat is cooked through and tender. Stir once during cooking.

To serve now: Taste to check you are happy with the seasoning. Spoon portions into warmed bowls, top with soured cream and serve with rice, if you like.

To freeze: Allow the remaining goulash to cool completely. Spoon portions into small polybags. Seal, label and freeze. Use within 4 months.

To serve from the freezer: Take out as many portions as required and put into a bowl, still in their bags. Defrost overnight in the fridge. Then pour into a saucepan, cover and bring slowly to the boil. Continue to cook, stirring, until piping hot.

This rich ruby-red stew is flavoured with paprika and originates from Hungary where it began as a meat and vegetable soup known as gulyás.

There's nothing better on a cold day than a rich beef stew braised in beer. This version is packed with extra flavour from the pancetta and chunks of carrot.

Warming Beef in Beer Stew

Makes 4 individual portions

Time 3 hours
Per portion: 542 Kcal
26g fat (9g saturated)

Preheat the oven to 160°C/325°F/Gas 3. Heat half the oil in a large flameproof casserole and cook the onions for about 5 minutes until softened.

Add the pancetta and cook for about 5 minutes until it starts to turn crispy, stirring occasionally. Remove the onions and pancetta from the casserole with a slotted spoon and set aside.

Toss the beef in the flour and cook in batches for about 10 minutes, until browned, adding the remaining oil as necessary.

Return the onions and pancetta to the casserole. Add the carrots, then pour in the beer, crumble in the stock cube and stir in the herbs. Season to taste. Slowly bring the mixture to the boil, stirring all the time.

Cover the casserole and bake in the oven for 2–2½ hours until the meat is tender. Stir halfway through.

To serve now: Spoon into warmed bowls and serve.

To freeze: Allow the remaining stew to cool completely. Spoon portions into small polybags. Seal, label and freeze. Use within 4 months.

To serve from the freezer: Take out as many portions as required and place in a bowl to defrost in the fridge overnight. Transfer to a small casserole and reheat in a preheated oven at 200°C/400°F/Gas 6 for 40–45 minutes, stirring after 20 minutes, until it is bubbling and hot all the way through. The cooking time will depend on the number of portions.

Sunflower oil 3 tbsp
Onions 2, peeled and chopped
Diced pancetta 2 x 77g packets
Lean braising steak 4 x 400g packets, diced
Plain flour 2 tbsp
Carrots 300g (11oz), peeled and cut into chunks
Beer, such as pale ale 750ml (1¼ pints)
Beef stock cube 1
Dried mixed herbs ½ tsp
Salt and freshly ground black pepper

Scan the **QR Code** with a smartphone for an ingredients shopping list

Makes 4

Cornish Pasties

Time 55 minutes
Per pasty: 630 Kcal
45g fat (16g saturated)

Potato 1, peeled and very finely diced

Carrot 1, peeled and very finely diced

Onion 1 small, peeled and very finely diced

Lean beef steak 225g (8oz), trimmed and cut into small pieces

Salt and freshly ground black pepper

Shortcrust pastry 450g (1lb)

Egg 1, beaten

Scan the **QR Code** with a smartphone for an ingredients shopping list

Mix together the potato, carrot, onion and steak and season well.

On a lightly floured surface roll out the pastry thinly. Cut three saucer-sized circles, then use the trimmings to make a fourth. Divide the meat and vegetables between each circle, and brush the edges with egg. Bring up the edges of each pasty to meet at the top. Crimp together the edges by pinching gently with your finger and thumb to seal.

To serve now: Preheat the oven to 220°C/425°F/Gas 7. Place the number you require on a baking sheet and brush all over with beaten egg. Bake for 10 minutes, then reduce the heat to 180°C/350°F/Gas 4 and cook for a further 15–20 minutes until golden and cooked through. Allow to cool for 10 minutes before serving.

To freeze: Open-freeze the remaining pasties on parchment paper on a baking sheet until solid, then take off the baking sheet, wrap in parchment paper and put into polybags. Seal, label and freeze. Use within 2 months.

To serve from freezer: Take the pasty out of its bag, keeping it in the paper, and thaw in the fridge overnight. Cook as above.

 You could double the quantities and make a batch of 8 for picnics and packed lunches.

These classic pasties are so simple to make yet make a delicious lunch or hearty meal when served with roasted vegetables.

A delicious alternative to a traditional cottage pie, this mildly spiced minced beef recipe is topped with velvety polenta and tangy Cheddar.

Beef & Polenta Pies

Makes 4 individual pies

Time 2 hours plus cooling
Per portion: 482 Kcal
22g fat (9g saturated)

Heat the oil in a large saucepan or frying pan and fry the onion with the mince, stirring, for 5-8 minutes, until the mince is evenly browned.

Stir in the chilli powder, cumin and garlic and fry for 2 minutes. Then add the tomatoes, stock, sugar, tomato purée and seasoning. Bring to the boil. Cover and simmer for 45 minutes, stirring occasionally.

Meanwhile, bring 800ml (28fl oz) of water to the boil and line a small roasting tin with foil brushed with oil.

Add the polenta to the water with 2 teaspoons of salt and cook for 5–10 minutes, stirring, until it is very thick. Mix in the butter and half of the cheese.

Spoon the polenta into the roasting tin, level with a wooden spoon or wetted hands and leave to cool.

Spoon the mince into four individual ovenproof or foil dishes. When cold, lift the foil and polenta out of the roasting tin. Cut into 12 triangles, remove the foil and arrange the triangles over the mince. Sprinkle the remaining cheese over the top.

To serve now: Preheat the oven to 200°C/400°F/Gas 6. Cook in the oven for 45 minutes until piping hot.

To freeze: Leave the remaining dishes to cool completely. Wrap with foil, seal, label and freeze. Use within 4 months.

To serve from the freezer: Take out as many portions as required. Defrost in the fridge overnight. Unwrap and cook as above.

Olive oil 1 tbsp
Onion 1, peeled and chopped
Minced beef 450g (1lb)
Hot chilli powder ½ tsp
Ground cumin 1 tsp
Garlic 1 clove, peeled and crushed
Chopped tomatoes 400g can
Beef stock 150ml (¼ pint)
Sugar 2 tsp
Tomato purée 2 tbsp
Salt and freshly ground black pepper
Quick cook polenta 200g (7oz)
Butter 25g (1oz)
Cheddar cheese 50g (2oz), grated

Scan the **QR Code** with a smartphone for an ingredients shopping list

Apple & Mint Sorbet

Makes 16 scoops

Time 30 minutes plus freezing
Per portion: 110 Kcal
0g fat (0g saturated)

Cooking apples 675g (1½lb), peeled and chopped
Granulated sugar 175g (6oz)
Powdered gelatine 2 tsp
Chopped mint 3 tbsp, plus extra leaves to serve

Scan the **QR Code** with a smartphone for an ingredients shopping list

Put the apples into a saucepan with 25g (1oz) of the sugar and 3 tablespoons of water. Cover with a lid and simmer for 10 minutes until the apples are soft.

Let it cool, then purée the apples in a liquidiser or press through a sieve.

Meanwhile, to make a syrup, put 3 tablespoons of water into a cup and sprinkle in the gelatine. Leave to soak for 5 minutes.

Put the remaining sugar into a saucepan with 450ml (¾ pint) of water. Slowly bring it to the boil, stirring occasionally until the sugar dissolves, then boil rapidly for 3 minutes.

Take the pan off the heat, add the gelatine and stir until it has dissolved. Leave to cool.

Stir the apple purée into the syrup together with the mint, then pour it into a shallow plastic box, cover and freeze for 4–5 hours until it is slushy. Beat with a fork or transfer to a liquidiser and blend until smooth. Return it to the container and leave to freeze completely for about four hours or overnight.

To serve from the freezer: Take out as many scoops as required and allow to thaw for 10 minutes before serving with fresh mint leaves, if you like.

Cook's TIPS
If you freeze the sorbet in a shallow metal non-stick cake tin you can reduce the freezing time to 3-4 hours. Beat well, then transfer to a plastic tub for the final freezing. It's delicious served with a ginger biscuit on the side.

Fresh mint might seem a surprising addition to sorbet, but it works wonderfully with the apple, giving a clean, fresh and totally delicious taste.

These cute little lemony biscuits are perfect as a mid-afternoon treat with a hot cuppa.

Lemon Swirl Biscuits

Makes 12-14 biscuits

Time 25 minutes
Per biscuit: 103 Kcal
7g fat (4g saturated)

Preheat the oven to 160°C/325°F/Gas 3 and line two baking sheets with non-stick baking paper or use non-stick baking sheets.

Cream together the butter and sugar. Sift in the flour and mix in with the grated lemon zest. Work in the lemon juice and mix again to a stiff biscuit mix.

Spoon the mixture into a piping bag fitted with a star nozzle and pipe small swirls onto the baking sheets, spaced well apart as they will spread. When you lift up the nozzle from piping each swirl, use a knife to trim the biscuit mixture neatly.

Bake in the oven for 12–15 minutes or until lightly golden and cooked.

To serve now: Leave the biscuits to cool on the baking sheets for about a minute then transfer to a wire rack with a palette knife to cool and firm up. They will keep in an airtight container for a few days.

To freeze: Carefully place the biscuits to be frozen in rigid plastic containers in a single layer or between sheets of greaseproof paper. Cover, seal and label. Use within 1 month.

To serve from the freezer: Thaw as many biscuits as required at room temperature on a wire rack for about an hour or until thoroughly defrosted.

Butter 110g (4oz), softened
Icing sugar 50g (2oz), sifted
Plain flour 125g (4½oz)
Lemon 1, grated zest and 1 tsp juice

Scan the **QR Code** with a smartphone for an ingredients shopping list

You can also freeze these biscuits before they are cooked. Open-freeze on baking paper on a baking tray and then pack into a plastic tub. Place frozen biscuits onto a baking tray and bake for 15-18 minutes at the same temperature as above.

Anzac Biscuits

Makes 20–24 biscuits

Time 30 minutes
Per biscuit: 61 Kcal
4g fat (3g saturated)

Butter 75g (3oz)
Golden syrup 2 tsp
Ground cinnamon ½ rounded tsp
Bicarbonate of soda ½ tsp
Caster sugar 50g (2oz)
Rolled oats 50g (2oz)
Plain flour 50g (2oz)
Desiccated coconut 50g (2oz)

Scan the **QR Code** with a smartphone for an ingredients shopping list

Preheat the oven to 150°C/300°F/Gas 2 and line two baking sheets with non-stick baking paper.

Melt the butter in a large pan with the syrup and cinnamon. When hot, add the bicarbonate of soda and 2 teaspoons of water. Stir well, then quickly add the sugar, oats, flour and coconut and mix well again. Put 10-12 heaped teaspoonfuls of the mixture on each baking sheet, spaced well apart.

Bake in the oven for 12–15 minutes or until lightly golden and cooked.

To serve now: Leave the biscuits to cool on the baking sheets for about 5 minutes, then transfer to a wire rack with a palette knife to cool and firm up. They will keep in an airtight container for a few days.

To freeze: Carefully place the biscuits to be frozen in rigid plastic containers in a single layer or between sheets of greaseproof paper. Cover, seal and label. Use within 3 months.

To serve from the freezer: Thaw as many biscuits as required at room temperature on a wire rack for about 30 minutes or until thoroughly defrosted. For a crisp biscuit, reheat for 5 minutes in the oven at 160°C/325°F/Gas 3.

Leave out the coconut and add chopped raisins instead. If you have a fan function on your oven, cook both trays of biscuits at once. With a conventional oven, swap the trays over after 10 minutes.

These syrupy, cinnamon biscuits are packed full of oats and are perfect for packing into a lunchbox for an energy boost while on a busy day out.

These moist citrus sponge slices are packed full of fruit and topped with crunchy demerara sugar.

Fruit Slices

Makes 16 slices

Time 1 hour
Per slice: 165 Kcal
7g fat (1.5g saturated)

Preheat the oven to 170°C/325°F/Gas 3 and grease and base line a small 18 x 28 x 4 cm (7 x 11 x 1½in) roasting tin with non-stick baking paper.

Put the margarine, caster sugar, flour, eggs, orange and lemon zest and milk into a bowl and beat with a wooden spoon or electric mixer until smooth. Stir in the fruit.

Spoon the mixture into the prepared tin, level the surface and sprinkle with the demerara sugar. Cook for 30 minutes until well risen and golden. The top of the cake will spring back when pressed with fingertips if it is ready.

To serve now: Leave the cake to cool in the tin. When it is cold take it out, peel off the paper and cut it into slices and arrange on a serving plate. The slices will keep in an airtight container for a few days.

To freeze: Carefully place the slices to be frozen in rigid plastic containers in a single layer or between sheets of greaseproof paper. Cover, seal and label. Use within 4 months.

To serve from the freezer: Thaw as many slices as required at room temperature on a wire rack for about 2 hours or until thoroughly defrosted.

Butter 150g (5oz), softened
Caster sugar 150g (5oz)
Self-raising flour 175g (6oz)
Eggs 2
Orange 1, grated zest
Lemon 1, grated zest
Milk 2 tbsp
Mixed dried fruit 175g (6oz)
Demerara sugar 2 tbsp

Scan the **QR Code** with a smartphone for an ingredients shopping list

Choose any combination of dried fruit you like. Use a standard mix, or try something more exotic, such as chopped mango and pineapple.

Makes 16 squares

Time 20 minutes plus chilling
Per square: 160 Kcal
7g fat (4g saturated)

Dark chocolate 150g (5oz), broken into pieces
Butter 50g (2oz)
Golden syrup 3 tbsp
Nice biscuits 200g (7oz)
Glacé ginger 1 tbsp
Sultanas 75g (3oz)

 Scan the **QR Code** with a smartphone for an ingredients shopping list

No-Bake Chocolate Squares

Line the base and sides of a shallow 18.5cm (7in) square tin with cling film.

Put the chocolate into a saucepan with the butter and syrup. Heat it gently, stirring occasionally, until it is melted.

Remove the chocolate mixture from the heat. Put the biscuits into a plastic bag and crush them into small pieces with a rolling pin.

Stir the biscuits, ginger and sultanas into the chocolate mixture until they are evenly coated.

Spoon into the tin, level the surface and chill for 2–3 hours.

To serve now: Lift the cling film out of the tin and peel it away. Cut the mixture into 16 squares. They will keep in an airtight container for a few days.

To freeze: Carefully place the squares to be frozen in rigid plastic containers in a single layer or between sheets of greaseproof paper. Cover, seal and label. Use within 1 month.

To serve from the freezer: Thaw as many slices as required at room temperature on a wire rack for about an hour or until thoroughly defrosted.

 Glacé ginger is sold ready chopped in the baking section of the supermarket. If it is unavailable use drained stem ginger and chop before mixing with the chocolate.

A real grown up treat. This easy chocolate bake is so moreish it won't hang around for long, so you might not need the freezer!

Once you have tasted these gorgeous blueberry bakes, you'll never buy a shop-made muffin again – they taste amazing.

Blueberry & Buttermilk Muffins

Makes 12 muffins

Time 45 minutes
Per muffin: 182 Kcal
8g fat (5g saturated)

Plain flour 300g (11oz)
Baking powder 2 tsp
Caster sugar 175g (6oz)
Blueberries 2 x 100g punnets
Buttermilk 284ml pot
Butter 100g (3½oz), melted and cooled
Eggs 2, beaten

Scan the **QR Code** with a smartphone for an ingredients shopping list

Preheat the oven to 190°C/375°F/Gas 5 and place paper cases in a 12-hole muffin tin.

Sift together the flour and baking powder in a large mixing bowl and stir in the sugar. Then add the blueberries and coat well in the flour mix to stop them from sinking to the bottom of the muffins.

In a separate bowl, whisk together the buttermilk, butter and eggs.

Add the buttermilk mixture to the mixing bowl and fold together until just combined, taking care not to overmix. Spoon into the paper cases.

Bake for 25–30 minutes or until risen, golden and firm to the touch.

To serve now: Cool in the tin for 5 minutes then place on a wire rack to cool completely.

To freeze: Carefully place the muffins to be frozen in rigid plastic containers in a single layer. Cover, seal and label. Use within 1 month.

To serve from the freezer: Thaw as many muffins as required at room termperature on a wire rack for 1–1½ hours. Warm through in the microwave for 10-15 seconds or in the oven for 8-10 minutes at 160°C/325°F/Gas 3.

Cook's TIPS

Buttermilk is the product left over after making butter. It can be found in the dairy chiller in the supermarket.

Buttermilk & Cinnamon Scones

Makes 10-12 scones

Time 25 minutes
Per scone: 220 Kcal
7g fat (4g saturated)

Self-raising flour 450g (1lb)
Baking powder ½ tsp
Ground cinnamon ¼-½ tsp
Caster sugar 75g (3oz)
Butter 100g (3½oz), diced
Buttermilk 284ml pot
Milk to glaze
Jam and clotted cream to serve (optional)

Scan the **QR Code** with a smartphone for an ingredients shopping list

Preheat the oven to 220°C/425°F/Gas 7 and line two baking sheets with non-stick baking paper.

Mix together the self-raising flour, baking powder, cinnamon and sugar in a bowl. Rub in the butter until the mixture resembles fine breadcrumbs.

Pour in enough buttermilk and mix with a knife to make a fairly stiff dough. Bring together with your hands and tip out onto a lightly floured work surface.

Pat the dough to 3cm (1¼in) thick. Using a 6.8cm (2¾in) diameter cutter dipped in flour, cut out 10–12 rounds, gathering up and re-rolling the trimmings.

Place the rounds, well spaced apart, on the baking sheets, brush the tops with a little milk, and bake for 10–15 minutes until well risen, firm and golden and sound hollow when tapped on the bottom.

Too serve now: Transfer the scones to a wire rack to cool. Serve warm with jam and clotted cream.

To freeze: Place the scones to be frozen in rigid plastic containers in a single layer. Cover, seal and label. Use within 1 month.

To serve from the freezer: Place as many scones as required on a wire rack and thaw at room temperature for about an hour and then warm through in the microwave for 10 to 15 seconds.

 If you prefer a stronger cinnamon taste, add more to the mixture in step two.

106 Eat & Freeze

These rich and creamy buttermilk scones will become a favourite recipe you turn to again and again.

These scones boast an unusual blend of flavours, which work wonderfully together. Serve warm with jam and clotted cream.

Ginger & Prune Scones

Makes 12 scones

Time 25 minutes
Per scone: 177 Kcal
3g fat (2g saturated)

Preheat the oven to 220°C/425°F/Gas 7 and line two baking sheets with non-stick baking paper.

Mix together all the ingredients except the butter and buttermilk or yogurt in a bowl. Then rub in the butter until the mixture resembles fine breadcrumbs.

Pour in the buttermilk or yogurt and mix with a knife to make a fairly stiff dough. Bring together with your hands and tip out onto a lightly floured work surface.

Pat the dough to 2.5cm (1in) thick. Using a 5cm (2in) diameter cutter dipped in flour, cut out 12 rounds, gathering up and re-rolling the trimmings.

Place the rounds well spaced apart on the baking sheets, brush the tops with a little milk, and bake for 12–15 minutes until well risen, firm and golden and sound hollow when tapped on the bottom.

To serve now: Transfer the scones to a wire rack to cool. Serve warm with jam and clotted cream.

To freeze: Place the scones to be frozen in rigid plastic containers in a single layer. Cover, seal and label. Use within 1 month.

To serve from the freezer: Place as many scones as required on a wire rack and thaw at room temperature for about an hour and then warm through in the microwave for 10 to 15 seconds.

Self-raising flour 175g (6oz)
Wholemeal flour 175g (6oz)
Baking powder 1 tbsp
Salt a good pinch
Dark soft brown sugar 75g (3oz)
Stem ginger 50g (2oz), drained and chopped
Ready-to-eat pitted prunes 75g (3oz), chopped
Butter 40g (1½oz), cut into small pieces
Buttermilk or natural yogurt 200ml (7fl oz)
Milk to glaze
Jam and clotted cream to serve (optional)

Scan the **QR Code** with a smartphone for an ingredients shopping list

Try different ready-to-eat dried fruits in place of the prunes; choose your favourite.

Eat & Freeze 109

Sticky Walnut Tart

Makes 8 slices

Time 1½ hours
Per portion: 476 Kcal
26g fat (5g saturated)

Plain flour 175g (6oz)
Salt a pinch
Butter 150g (5oz), diced
Light muscovado sugar 175g (6oz)
Golden syrup 225g (8oz)
Eggs 3 medium
Vanilla essence 1 tsp
Walnut pieces 110g (4oz)
Vanilla ice cream to serve (optional)

Scan the **QR Code** with a smartphone for an ingredients shopping list

To make the pastry, put the flour and salt into a bowl. Then add 75g (3oz) of the butter and rub it in with your fingertips until fine crumbs form.

Mix to a soft but not sticky dough with 2 tablespoons of water. Knead lightly and roll out the pastry onto a floured surface to a circle a little larger than a 23cm (9in) loose-bottomed flan tin.

Lift the pastry over the rolling pin, transfer it to the flan tin and press it onto the base and up the sides with your fingertips. Trim the top and chill in the fridge while you make the filling.

Put the remaining butter, sugar and golden syrup into a saucepan and heat it until the butter melts and the sugar has dissolved. Allow it to cool.

Preheat the oven to 190°C/375°F/Gas 5. Beat the eggs and vanilla essence together, then gradually stir it into the syrup mixture with the walnuts. Pour it into the flan case, place on a baking sheet and bake for 35 minutes until it is just set in the centre (check after 20 minutes and cover with foil if browning too quickly).

To serve now: Allow the tart to cool slightly, then remove it from the tin and transfer it to a serving plate. Serve with ice cream if you like.

To freeze: Cut the tart into individual slices, wrap in cling film, seal and label. Freeze for up to 2 months.

To serve from the freezer: Take out as many slices as required and defrost at room temperature for 2 hours or until completely defrosted.

A crisp, delicious sticky tart with a chewy walnut centre – wonderful served with a scoop of vanilla ice cream.

Homemade is always best, and this delightful Swiss roll is no exception. Small, but perfectly formed, its fluffy sponge is filled with delicious raspberry jam.

Raspberry Swiss Roll

Makes 8 slices

Time 30 minutes
Per slice: 167 Kcal
3g fat (1g saturated)

Preheat the oven to 200°C/400°F/Gas 6 and line a 33 x 22cm (13 x 9in) tray bake tin with non-stick baking paper.

Use an electric mixer to whisk the eggs and sugar for about 7 minutes until thick and creamy enough to leave a good trail from the whisk.

Fold in the flour and 1 tablespoon of warm water. Pour the mixture into the tin, letting it find its own level. Bake for 12–14 minutes until firm to touch.

Meanwhile, place a sheet of non-stick baking paper on a clean damp cloth. Sprinkle the paper with caster sugar. Warm the jam in a saucepan.

Turn the cake out straightaway onto the paper. Peel off the paper and trim the edges all round. Spread the warm jam over the cake, almost to the edges. Make a short cut, about a thumb's width up from the short edge nearest you then quickly roll the cake up from there, discarding the paper as you work.

Hold the cake in position for half a minute then transfer it, join-side down, to a wire rack to cool.

To serve now: Dredge with more caster sugar, slice and serve with fresh raspberries, if you like.

To freeze: When the cake is cold, interleave the slices to be frozen with paper, then put them in a polybag, label and freeze. Use within 3 months.

To serve from the freezer: Remove the wrappings and thaw at room temperature. The whole cake will take 2 hours and the slices about 1 hour to thaw.

Eggs 3 large
Caster sugar 110g (4oz), plus a little extra for dredging
Plain flour 75g (3oz)
Raspberry jam 6 tbsp
Raspberries to serve (optional)

Scan the **QR Code** with a smartphone for an ingredients shopping list

Makes 8-10 slices

Banana & Sultana Loaf

Time 1½ hours plus standing
Per slice: 176 Kcal
0.4g fat (0g saturated)

Sultanas 225g (8oz)
Hot tea 300ml (½ pint)
Sunflower oil for brushing
Bananas 200g (7oz) weight with skins on
Light brown or caster sugar 110g (4oz)
Self-raising flour 225g (8oz)
Bicarbonate of soda 1 tsp
Ground cinnamon 1 tsp

Scan the **QR Code** with a smartphone for an ingredients shopping list

Put the sultanas in a bowl and pour over the hot tea. Leave for 1 hour.

Preheat the oven to 180°C/350°F/Gas 4. Lightly brush a 900g (2lb) loaf tin with a little oil and line the base with non-stick baking paper.

Peel and mash the bananas in a large bowl. Add the sugar, flour, bicarbonate of soda and cinnamon, then stir in the sultanas and tea and mix thoroughly.

Spoon the mixture into the tin, level the surface and cook for about 1 hour or until well risen and a skewer comes out cleanly when inserted in the cake.

To serve now: Leave the cake to cool in the tin, then loosen the edges and turn out, peel off the paper and slice.

To freeze: When the cake is cold, interleave the slices to be frozen with paper, then put them in a polybag, label and freeze. Use within 3 months.

To serve from the freezer: Thaw as many slices as required at room temperature for about 2 hours or until thoroughly defrosted.

You can use luxury mixed fruits in place of the sultanas, if you prefer.

It tastes really good spread with a little butter.

Moist, with just a hint of banana, this classic tea loaf is scrumptious spread with a little butter.

A fabulous yellow-hued fruit bread, which originates from Cornwall where saffron was once traded for Cornish tin. Serve cold spread with butter or lightly toasted.

Cornish Saffron Cake

Makes 8–10 slices

Time 1½ hours plus standing
Per slice: 339 Kcal
12g fat (6g saturated)

Butter a 900g (2lb) loaf tin. Place the saffron on a sheet of non-stick baking paper and put it in a coolish oven for a few minutes to dry out. Crumble the saffron into a small bowl, pour over 2 tablespoons boiling water and leave to steep for at least 1 hour.

Tip the flour into a bowl and then rub in the butter and lard until it resembles breadcrumbs. Stir in the salt, currants, mixed peel, caster sugar and yeast.

Beat together the eggs, milk, almond essence and steeped saffron. Pour the liquid into the flour mixture and mix well to form a soft dough.

Turn the dough out onto a floured surface and knead it for about 10 minutes until it's smooth and elastic. Shape the dough into a loaf and place in the tin. Cover with a sheet of oiled cling film and leave it in a warm place until it has doubled in size.

Preheat the oven to 200°C/400°F/Gas 6. Cook the loaf in the centre of the oven for 20 minutes, then reduce the oven temperature to 180°C/350°F/Gas 4 and cook for a further 20–30 minutes or until the loaf has risen and feels hollow when tapped underneath when taken out of the tin.

To serve now: Remove the loaf from the oven and transfer it to a wire rack to cool before slicing.

To freeze: Once cooled, place the loaf in a polybag, label and freeze. Use within 3 months.

To serve from the freezer: Thaw at room temperature for about 2 hours or until defrosted.

Dried strands of saffron a large pinch
Strong plain flour 450g (1lb)
Butter 75g (3oz)
Lard 40g (1½oz)
Salt a large pinch
Currants 200g (7oz)
Cut mixed peel 50g (2oz)
Caster sugar 2 tbsp
Fast-action dried yeast 7g sachet
Eggs 2
Milk 125ml (4fl oz), luke warm
Almond essence a few drops

Scan the **QR Code** with a smartphone for an ingredients shopping list

Makes 16–20 squares

Chocolate Fudgey Cake

Time 1¼ hours
Per square: 202 Kcal
11g fat (3g saturated)

Cocoa powder 75g (3oz)
Eggs 3
Light muscovado sugar 250g (9oz)
Olive oil or rapeseed oil 125ml (4fl oz)
Self-raising flour 150g (5oz)
Bicarbonate of soda 1 tsp
Dark chocolate 150g (5oz), broken into chunks
Butter 25g (1oz)
Milk 4 tbsp
Golden syrup 1 tbsp
Milk chocolate 50g (2oz), broken into pieces and melted in a bowl over a pan of hot water

Scan the **QR Code** with a smartphone for an ingredients shopping list

Whisk 50g (2oz) cocoa powder with 100ml (3½fl oz) boiling water in a small bowl until smooth. Leave to cool for a few minutes.

Preheat the oven to 180°C/350°F/Gas 4 and line a 33 x 22cm (13 x 9in) tray bake tin with non-stick baking paper.

In a large bowl whisk the eggs, sugar and oil for 3 minutes, until smooth, using an electric whisk.

Mix in the flour, bicarbonate of soda and cocoa paste. Pour into the tin and allow to settle.

Bake for 35-40 minutes until the cake is risen and a skewer inserted comes out clean. Leave for 10 minutes, then turn out onto a wire rack to cool.

To make the icing, melt the dark chocolate with the butter in a bowl over a pan of barely simmering water and stir until smooth. At the same time, mix the remaining cocoa powder, milk and syrup in a pan and heat until almost boiling. Whisk it into the chocolate mixture to make a glossy icing.

Smooth the icing over the cake, drizzle with the milk chocolate and leave to set. Cut into squares.

To serve now: Enjoy the cakes and keep any extras in an airtight container for a few days.

To freeze: Place in rigid plastic containers in a single layer or between sheets of greaseproof paper. Cover, seal and label. Use within 2 months.

To serve from the freezer: Thaw at room temperature for about 2 hours or until defrosted.

A really grown up chocolate cake, which goes perfectly with a hot mug of coffee, or even a cheeky glass of red wine!

Eat Out, In

Mushrooms with Goat's Cheese	122	
Prawn Cocktail Pasta	125	
Speedy Spicy Scallops	126	
Lemon & Thyme Roast Poussin and Potatoes	129	
Pork Parcels	130	
Antipasti Pitta Pizza	133	
Fillet Steak with Chimichurri Sauce	134	
Creamy Monkfish & Cauliflower Curry	137	
Pan-Fried Sea Bass & Scallops with Hollandaise Sauce	138	
Sea Bass Spanish-Style	141	
Gingery Prawn Stir-Fry	142	
Chicken & Sweet Potato with Herby Sauce	145	
Spring Chicken in Broth with Minted Pea Purée	146	
Mini Moussakas	149	
Griddled Lamb with Fresh Pesto, Celeriac Mash & Ratatouille	150	
Beef Steak with Peppercorn Sauce & Potato Wedges	153	
Fresh Fruit with Chocolate Dip	154	
Roasted Strawberries with Lemon Ripple	157	
Peach & Ginger Pavlova	158	
Lemon Posset	161	
Portuguese Baked Custards	162	
Apricots Baked in Buttermilk Custard	165	
Crêpes with Brandy Marmalade Sauce	166	
Apricot Bakewell Tarts	169	
Plum Tarts	170	

Serves 1

Mushrooms with Goat's Cheese

Time 40 minutes
Per portion: 185 Kcal
12g fat (7g saturated)

Large flat mushroom 1, wiped
Shallot 1, peeled and finely chopped
Fresh white breadcrumbs 15g (½oz)
Butter 15g (½oz), melted
Chopped thyme 1 tsp, plus leaves to garnish
Salt and freshly ground black pepper
Goat's cheese 25g round slice
Salad leaves to serve (optional)

 Scan the **QR Code** with a smartphone for an ingredients shopping list

Preheat the oven to 200°C/400°F/Gas 6. Remove the stalk from the mushroom. Chop the stalk finely and then mix with the shallot, breadcrumbs, melted butter, thyme and seasoning.

Pack the mixture into the mushroom. Place on a baking sheet and cook in the centre of the oven for 15 minutes.

Place the cheese on the mushroom and sprinkle with a few extra thyme leaves. Return to the oven for a further 10–15 minutes, or until the cheese starts to melt and turn golden. Remove from the oven, sprinkle with black pepper and serve immediately with a few salad leaves if liked.

Mushrooms don't need peeling; just wipe with a clean, damp cloth or small mushroom brush to remove any dirt.

This recipe is ideal fo using up any leftover cheese; instead of goat's cheese use any sliced soft cheese or grated hard cheese of your choice.

You could use a pinch of dried thyme instead of fresh.

You could also add a little lemon zest to the stuffing mixture if you like.

This superb starter combines the rich velvety texture of goat's cheese with earthy mushrooms, which are packed with a crunchy thyme-flavoured filling.

This suprising combination of classic prawn cocktail and pasta works beautifully. The tangy dressing and succulent prawns provide the perfect complement to the linguine.

Prawn Cocktail Pasta

 Serves 1

Time 15 minutes
Per portion: 465 Kcal
17g fat (10g saturated)

Cook the pasta in a saucepan of boiling water for according to the packet's instructions.

Meanwhile, mix the tomato purée, crème fraîche, Worcestershire sauce, tabasco and lemon juice together in a bowl.

Drain the pasta, put it back in the pan, on a low heat, add the sauce and prawns and warm through. Then tear in the lettuce leaves and serve in a warmed bowl, dusted with paprika.

Dried linguine 75g (3oz)

Tomato purée 2 tsp

Crème fraîche 2–3 tbsp

Worcestershire sauce a few dashes

Tabasco a good dash

Lemon 2 tsp juice

Cooked and peeled coldwater prawns 75g (3oz), defrosted, if frozen

Little Gem leaves 3–4

Paprika for sprinkling

 Scan the **QR Code** with a smartphone for an ingredients shopping list

Use whichever pasta you have.

Use tomato ketchup if you don't have purée, adding a little more lemon juice.

Crème fraîche is good to have in the fridge for instant sauces for pasta or for fish or chicken with the addition of a little lemon juice and some torn herbs.

Any leftover lettuce can be cooked with a few frozen peas in vegetable stock to make soup.

Serves 1

Speedy Spicy Scallops

Time 15 minutes
Per portion: 288 Kcal
13g fat (2g saturated)

Olive oil 1 tbsp

Large scallops 5, with or without roe, trimmed and halved

Garlic 1 clove, peeled and sliced

Peeled and grated root ginger 1 tsp

Small red chilli 1, deseeded and chopped

Sugar snap peas a good handful

Pak choi 1, leaves separated and thickly sliced

Salt and freshly ground black pepper

Coriander leaves a good handful

Lime ½, juice only

Heat the oil in a frying pan over a hot heat. Add the scallops and the roe (if using) and fry for a minute or until just turning golden underneath. Then flip them over and add the garlic, ginger, chilli, sugar snap peas and pak choi. Cook for another minute.

Season with salt and pepper, then scatter with coriander leaves and lime juice and serve.

 Scan the **QR Code** with a smartphone for an ingredients shopping list

This recipe would be great with prawns or squid instead of scallops or try a mixture of shellfish.

Buy frozen packs of scallops and prawns and keep them in the freezer for quick special meals as they take little time to thaw.

You could serve with sautéed potatoes, chips, rice or noodles, if you like.

Season with Thai fish sauce if you have some.

Mildly spiced, tender scallops with crunchy sugar snaps and pak choi – a quick and easy treat!

Sunday roasts don't have to be reserved for large gatherings. With a poussin and a potato, enjoy a delicious roast lunch for one.

Lemon & Thyme Roast Poussin and Potatoes

 Serves 1

Time 1¼ hours
Per portion: 596 Kcal
40g fat (9g saturated)

Preheat the oven to 200°C/400°F/Gas 6.

Add the potato to a pan of boiling water, bring back to the boil and simmer for 5 minutes.

Drain the potatoes, then shake them in the pan to rough up the edges a little.

Meanwhile, place 2 teaspoons of the oil in a small roasting tin, pop the tin in the oven and heat for about 5 minutes.

Add the potatoes to the hot oil, using a long-handled spoon – watch out as the oil will splatter. Baste the potatoes in the oil, season well then push them to the edge of the tin.

Place the poussin in the centre of the tin. Drizzle with a teaspoon of oil and sprinkle generously with the thyme and salt and pepper.

Roast the poussin and potatoes for 25 minutes. Then scatter the lemon zest and juice over the poussin and baste it with any juices from the tin.

Return to the oven and roast for a further 20–25 minutes or until the poussin is cooked through (see the tip, below) and the potatoes are crisp.

Transfer the poussin to a warmed serving plate and serve with any juices from the tin, the roast potatoes and fine green beans.

Potato 1 large, peeled and cut into chunks
Olive oil 1 tbsp
Salt and freshly ground black pepper
Poussin 1, preferably corn-fed
Dried thyme a large pinch
Lemon 1, grated zest and juice
Fine green beans 110g (4oz), trimmed, to serve

Scan the **QR Code** with a smartphone for an ingredients shopping list

Cook's TIPS

The exact cooking time will depend on the size. Pierce the thickest part of the thigh and check the juices run clear.

Instead of poussin, you could use a chicken breast joint on the bone or a chicken thigh and leg joint.

Serves 1

Pork Parcels

Time 35 minutes
Per parcel: 226 Kcal
10g fat (4g saturated)

Olive oil 1 tbsp plus 2 tsp

Pork tenderloin 110g (4oz) piece

Filo pastry 1 sheet

Bottled red pimiento peppers 2 pieces, well drained

Low fat garlic and herb soft cheese 25g (1oz)

Roasted cherry tomatoes and green beans to serve (optional)

 Scan the **QR Code** with a smartphone for an ingredients shopping list

Preheat the oven to 200°C/400°F/Gas 6. Heat 1 tablespoon oil in a non-stick frying pan, add the pork and fry over a high heat for 5 minutes, turning until evenly browned on all sides. Leave to cool.

Cut the sheet of filo in half, brush half with oil and then place the other half at an angle over the first. Put one piece of pimiento in the centre of the pastry and then place the piece of pork on top. Top with soft cheese and add another piece of pimiento.

Gather the pastry up and over the pork stack and pinch together to seal. Transfer to a baking sheet.

Brush the pork parcel with a little extra oil and then bake for 20–25 minutes until the pastry is golden and the pork is thoroughly cooked. Serve with roasted cherry tomatoes and green beans if liked.

 Cook's TIPS

Freeze the remaining filo pastry for use in the future.

The bottled peppers will keep for ages; add to salads or serve with cooked meat or fish.

Use any leftover soft cheese to top a baked potato, stir into pasta or spoon into an omelette. It can also be mixed with canned salmon, wrapped in filo and baked for 10 minutes.

Who needs to eat out when you can enjoy food like this at home? Simple to create, but this dish looks and tastes fabulous.

The authentic taste of Italy from your own kitchen – this delicious pizza is packed full of flavour and is made in just minutes.

Antipasti Pitta Pizza

 Serves 1

Time 15 minutes
Per portion: 484 Kcal
22g fat (8g saturated)

Preheat the grill to hot with the rack about 10cm (4in) away from the heat. Put the pitta on a baking sheet and grill on one side, just to warm it through.

Turn it over and spread with the pesto and about two-thirds of the cheese.

Tear the ham into a few strips straight over the top. Nestle in the artichoke pieces and tomato halves and sprinkle with the rest of the cheese. Drizzle a little oil from the jar of artichokes over the pizza.

Grill for about 5 minutes until the cheese has melted and browned. Season with pepper and sprinkle with basil leaves, if using.

Pitta bread 1
Pesto sauce 1 tbsp
Grated Mozzarella cheese 50g (2oz) or 5 heaped tbsp
Parma ham 1–2 slices
Chargrilled artichokes in olive oil 4 pieces
Cherry tomatoes 5–6, halved
Freshly ground black pepper
Basil leaves to garnish (optional)

Scan the **QR Code** with a smartphone for an ingredients shopping list

Cook's TIPS

Keep a pack of pitta breads in the freezer for quick thawing and toasting to serve for lunch or supper.

Fresh chilled pesto generally has a better flavour than that of an ambient jar, so buy that if you can. It will keep for a couple of weeks in the fridge as long as you ensure the top is covered with a thin layer of olive oil. Add it to pasta or crushed potatoes, or serve with fish or grilled chicken to use it up.

Ready-grated Mozzarella is very handy and will keep in the bag (250g pack) in the fridge 2–3 weeks.

Parma ham keeps well and can be quickly crisped in a pan to serve with scrambled egg instead of cooking bacon or on top of soups.

Fillet Steak with Chimichurri Sauce

 Serves 1

Time 1 hour
Per portion: 684 Kcal
51g fat (11g saturated)

Red chilli 1, deseeded and chopped

Garlic 2 cloves, peeled and finely chopped

Chopped curly parsley 2–3 tbsp

Dried oregano ½ tsp

Salt and freshly ground black pepper

Red wine vinegar 2 tbsp

Olive oil 5 tbsp

Small new potatoes 150g (5oz), scrubbed

Fillet steak 1

Olive oil 1 tsp

Leafy salad to serve (optional)

 Scan the **QR Code** with a smartphone for an ingredients shopping list

Preheat the oven to 200°C/400°F/Gas 6.

To make the sauce, mix together the chopped chilli, garlic, parsley and oregano with a pinch of salt and the vinegar and 2 tablespoons of the oil. Cover and leave to stand for about 30 minutes.

Meanwhile, add the potatoes to a pan of boiling water, cover with a lid, then reduce the heat and simmer for 5 minutes until just tender.

Drain the potatoes then tip into a roasting tin, drizzle with 2 tablespoons of the oil and season. Cook in the oven for about 30 minutes until tender, basting them in the oil halfway through.

Meanwhile, cook the steak. Heat a griddle until hot and brush both sides of the steaks with oil then season to taste. Add the steak to the grill and cook according to taste. Usually, for rare, 3–4 minutes on each side and for medium, 5–7 minutes on each side, but the exact cooking time depends on the thickness of the steak.

Transfer to a warm plate, cover with foil and leave to rest for 5 minutes (see tip, below).

Drizzle the steak with the sauce and serve with the potatoes and a side salad if using. Place any leftover sauce in a small bowl alongside.

 It is important to let the steak rest for about 5 minutes before serving, to allow the juices that have been drawn to the surface to relax back into the meat.

Treat yourself to a hearty steak served with this gorgeous sauce, made from chilli, garlic and herbs.

This decadent, creamy curry, packed full of flavoursome fish and tender cauliflower, beats a take-away hands down. Enjoy it with warmed naan bread on the side.

Creamy Monkfish & Cauliflower Curry

Serves 2

Time 20 mins
Per portion: 293 Kcal
14g fat (7g saturated)

Melt the butter in a saucepan and add the onion, ginger and garlic. Cook until soft.

Add the cauliflower, fish, turmeric and curry paste and cook for 2 minutes, stirring. Add the milk, bring up to the boil, cover and simmer for 5 minutes.

Mix the soft cheese with a little of the hot milk then pour into the pan. Stir and heat gently until piping hot. Sprinkle with coriander and serve with naan bread, if you like.

Butter 15g (½oz)

Onion 1, peeled and sliced

Root ginger 1cm (½in) piece, peeled and chopped

Garlic 1 clove, peeled and crushed

Cauliflower 200g (7oz), broken into florets

Monkfish or cod loin 225g (8oz), cubed

Turmeric ¼ tsp

Korma curry paste 1 tsp

Milk 200ml (7fl oz)

Low fat soft cheese with chives 50g (2oz)

Chopped coriander to garnish (optional)

Naan bread to serve (optional)

Scan the **QR Code** with a smartphone for an ingredients shopping list

Cook's TIPS

Monkfish or cod loin are quite meaty white fish, and work perfectly in this dish. You could use any white fish, but it might disintegrate slightly while cooking.

Spoon leftover soft cheese into homemade soups or onto a wrap with a slice or two of ham.

Serves 2

Time 15 minutes
Per portion: 751 Kcal
59g fat (31g saturated)

Pan-Fried Sea Bass & Scallops with Hollandaise Sauce

Sea bass fillets 2
Salt and freshly ground black pepper
Butter 25g (1oz)
Olive oil 1 tbsp
Scallops 6, trimmed
Hollandaise sauce half a 200ml pot, to serve
Samphire 90g packet, to serve

Scan the **QR Code** with a smartphone for an ingredients shopping list

Slash the skin of the sea bass with a sharp knife and season with salt and pepper.

Heat half the butter and oil in each of two separate frying pans. When foaming, add the sea bass fillets, skin-side down, to one pan. Hold down with a metal spatula to stop the fillets from curling up. Cook for 2–3 minutes or until the skin is crispy and golden and the flesh has turned white all the way round.

Meanwhile, season the scallops and add to the other pan. Cook for 4–5 minutes until cooked through, turning once; the exact cooking time depends on the thickness of the scallops.

Carefully turn the sea bass and cook for a further 1–2 minutes, then check the fish is cooked through. Again, the exact cooking time will depend on the thickness of the fish fillets.

Separately heat the Hollandaise sauce and the samphire, according to the packet's instructions.

Spoon a little Hollandaise sauce onto warmed plates, arrange the samphire in the centre and set a sea bass fillet on top. Garnish with the scallops and serve at once.

You can buy samphire in packets at the fish counter of your supermarket.

To use the remaining Hollandaise sauce, serve it with the steak on page 153 instead of the peppercorn sauce.

Salty vibrant green samphire is perfect with the sea bass and scallops in this recipe, which is served on creamy piquant Hollandaise.

Hearty, colourful and full of fabulous flavour, this is a quick and delicious meal – and you only have one pan to wash!

Sea Bass Spanish-Style

 *Serves 2*

Time 20 minutes
Per portion: 434 Kcal
25g fat (6g saturated)

Heat a deep frying pan, add the chorizo slices in one layer and fry for 3–4 minutes until browned on the underside then flip them over and brown the other side. Add the garlic and fennel seeds, then the courgette and kale. Stir-fry for about 5 minutes.

Add the butter beans, peppers and ketchup with 2 tablespoons of water. Cook for a few minutes until hot, then tip out into a warmed dish.

Slash the skin of the sea bass with a sharp knife, rub with oil and season with salt and pepper. Reheat the frying pan over a medium-high heat and sear the fish, skin-side down, for a couple of minutes. When the skin is crisp, flip the fish over and cook for a further 1–2 minutes or until the skin is crispy and the flesh has turned white all the way round.

Serve the fish on the vegetables drizzled with the pan juices.

Chorizo sausage 75g (3oz), cut into 12 slices
Garlic 1 clove, peeled and sliced
Fennel seeds 1 tsp
Courgette 1, trimmed and diced
Kale 110g (4oz), chopped
Butter beans 200g can, rinsed and drained
Peppadew peppers 6, halved and deseeded
Tomato ketchup 1 rounded tbsp
Olive oil 2 tbsp
Sea bass fillets 2
Salt and freshly ground black pepper

 Scan the **QR Code** with a smartphone for an ingredients shopping list

 Buy fresh sea bass or keep a pack of ready frozen sea bass on hand for quick suppers as they take so little time to thaw. You can also use any other fish you fancy.

Chorizo keeps for a few weeks in the fridge – add fried slices to pasta, risottos or soups for fabulous flavour.

If you don't have fennel seeds, don't worry. Add fresh chopped fennel leaves or parsley, at the end of cooking.

Peppadew peppers are small red peppers sold in jars. They are great to keep in the fridge for adding a quick shot of colour and heat to pasta, pizzas or veggie dishes.

Use robust spinach instead of kale if you like.

Kale keeps well for a week in the fridge. Wash it well and take out the thick stalks before adding to the pan.

 *Serves 2*

Gingery Prawn Stir-Fry

Time 20 minutes
Per portion: 723 Kcal
14g fat (1.5g saturated)

Vegetable oil 2 tbsp

Garlic 1 clove, peeled and sliced

Root ginger 4cm (2in) piece, peeled and cut into slivers

Carrot 1, peeled and cut into thin strips

Runner beans or green beans 110g (4oz), finely sliced

Spring onions 4, trimmed and each cut into 4 pieces

Raw peeled king prawns 200g (7oz)

Dried Thai rice noodles 2 x 125g (4½oz) sheaths

Sherry 4 tbsp

Soy sauce 3 tbsp

Spring greens 1 head, thick stalk removed, leaves shredded

 Scan the **QR Code** with a smartphone for an ingredients shopping list

Heat the oil in a wok with the garlic and ginger and stir-fry for half a minute. Add the carrot and fry for a minute. Stir in the beans, spring onions and prawns and stir-fry for a further 2 minutes.

Meanwhile, soak the rice noodles in boiling water as directed on the packet. Drain well.

Add the sherry and soy sauce to the wok, then pour in 250ml (8fl oz) boiling water. Bring to the boil and add the noodles. Bring back to the boil and spread the greens over the top. Cook for 2 minutes, stirring all the time.

Leave to stand for a minute for the noodles to absorb some more water, then serve straight from the wok.

 Use a small bean slicer gadget for speed and to get the beans all about the same width.

For the spring greens, cut a V-shape around the stalk to remove it from the leaves, then pile the halved leaves on top of each other and cut them into strips.

Who needs a trip to the local Chinese restaurant when you can make food this good at home?

Soft roasted sweet potatoes and tender chicken are the perfect comfort food – the herby sauce makes them even better.

Chicken & Sweet Potato with Herby Sauce

 *Serves 2*

Time 1½ hours
Per portion: 638 Kcal
28g fat (6g saturated)

Mix half of the lemon juice, 1 clove of garlic, 4 thyme sprigs and 1 tablespoon of the oil in a shallow dish. Add the drumsticks and coat them with the marinade. Cover and leave for 20–30 minutes (or longer) in the fridge.

Preheat the oven to 200°C/400°F/Gas 6 and put two baking trays in the oven to heat up.

Toss the potato wedges in 1 tablespoon of the oil to coat well. Add the rosemary leaves from the sprig and spread out the wedges on one of the hot baking trays. Roast for 45 minutes–1 hour, until tender.

Meanwhile put the drumsticks with the marinade on the other hot tray and cook for 45–50 minutes until they are browned and cooked through. Let them rest while the potatoes finish cooking.

Make the herb sauce by mixing the remaining lemon juice and zest, oil, garlic, chopped thyme and parsley together. Serve the hot wedges on warmed plates with the drumsticks and the herb sauce to spoon over.

Lemon 1, grated zest and juice

Garlic 2 cloves, peeled and crushed

Thyme 4 sprigs plus 1 tsp chopped

Olive oil 3 tbsp

Chicken drumsticks 6, skin scored a couple of times on each side

Sweet potato 1 (about 350g/12oz), unpeeled or peeled if you prefer, cut into wedges

Rosemary 1 large sprig

Chopped parsley 1 tbsp

 Scan the **QR Code** with a smartphone for an ingredients shopping list

 Cook's TIPS

A mixture of Maris Piper and sweet potato wedges looks and tastes good too.

Instead of drumsticks, cook a whole chicken leg, or 2 drumsticks and 1 thigh per person.

If you don't have time to marinate the chicken, don't worry, the dish still tastes good.

Serves 2

Spring Chicken in Broth with Minted Pea Purée

Time 1 hour
Per portion: 599 Kcal
29g fat (6g saturated)

Olive oil 2 tsp

Boneless, skinless chicken thighs 4

Young carrots 2, quartered

New potatoes 5, halved or cut into thick slices

French beans 10, trimmed and cut into thumb lengths

Hot chicken stock 600ml (1 pint)

Bay leaf 1

Spring greens 1 small head, leaves separated

Peas 50g (2oz) fresh or frozen

Mint leaves 10

Salt and freshly ground black pepper

 Scan the **QR Code** with a smartphone for an ingredients shopping list

Heat the oil in a deep-sided frying pan over a medium heat. Add the chicken and fry for about 5 minutes until browned well. Turn them over and cook for another 4–5 minutes.

Remove the chicken from the pan with a slotted spoon and set aside. Tip out the cooking juices into a small pan and set aside too.

Put the large pan back on the heat, add the carrots, potatoes and beans then put the chicken back on top. Pour in enough stock to cover the vegetables and chicken. Add the bay leaf. Bring to the boil, then reduce the heat and simmer very gently, uncovered, for 25 minutes until the chicken is just cooked.

Tear in the large spring green leaves and add the smaller leaves whole and simmer for another 5 minutes until the greens are just wilted.

Meanwhile, add the peas to the small pan containing the cooking juices. Add the mint leaves and 5 tablespoons of the stock from the chicken pan. Simmer for 5–8 minutes until softened. Mash to a rough purée and season well.

Serve the vegetables with the chicken in warmed bowls. Reduce the stock over a high heat for a minute or so (but it is meant to be a broth), then pour it into the bowls and top with the pea purée.

 Add some sliced leek or spring onions as well, if you like, or curly kale or spinach instead of the spring greens.

The show-stopping flavours in this dish will make you want to cook it again and again – it really is top-notch restaurant quality.

Capture the fragrance and taste of a Greek restaurant in your own kitchen with these authentic little moussaka dishes.

Mini Moussakas

 Serves 2

Time 1¼ hours
Per portion: 629 Kcal
42g fat (17g saturated)

Heat 1 teaspoon of the oil in a frying pan over a medium heat. Add the onion and garlic and cook for about 5 minutes until just beginning to brown. Increase the heat to high and add the lamb mince and fry for 3–4 minutes until browned.

Stir in the tomatoes, cinnamon and oregano with plenty of seasoning, reduce the heat and simmer gently for 20 minutes.

Meanwhile, preheat the grill to hot. Cut the aubergine across into 18 thin slices, lay them out on a baking sheet and brush them lightly on both sides with the rest of the oil. Grill the slices until browning on one side, then turn them over to soften.

Preheat the oven to 200°C/400°F/Gas 6 and have two 500ml (18fl oz) gratin dishes ready. Lay three aubergine slices in each dish, spoon a quarter of the mince mixture into each, add three more aubergine slices, the rest of the mince and then the last slices.

Beat the egg in a jug, beat in the cornflour and then beat in the yogurt. Season well and pour the sauce over the top of the dishes, then sprinkle with the Parmesan cheese.

Put the dishes on a baking tray and bake for 25–30 minutes until the moussakas are bubbling and golden. Serve with salad or green vegetables.

Olive oil 2 tbsp
Onion 1 small, peeled and chopped
Garlic 1 clove, peeled and crushed
Lamb mince 250g (9oz)
Chopped tomatoes 227g can
Ground cinnamon ½ tsp
Chopped oregano 1 tbsp (or 1 tsp if dried)
Salt and freshly ground black pepper
Aubergine 1, trimmed
Egg 1
Cornflour 1 tsp
Natural yogurt 150ml pot
Grated Parmesan cheese 4 tbsp
Salad leaves or green vegetables to serve (optional)

Scan the **QR Code** with a smartphone for an ingredients shopping list

Cook's TIPS

Make this in one dish if you prefer.

For even greater flavour, add some grated courgette to the mince mixture, or if you have some spinach in the fridge, wilt it down in a pan or the microwave and spread it on top of the first layer of mince.

Griddled Lamb with Fresh Pesto, Celeriac Mash & Ratatouille

 *Serves 2*

Time 45 minutes
Per portion: 659 Kcal
57g fat (17g saturated)

Celeriac 350g (12oz), peeled and diced

Lemon juice 3 tsp

Salt and freshly ground black pepper

Olive oil 4 tbsp

Red onion 1 small, peeled and sliced

Fennel 1 small head, cored and thinly sliced

Courgette 1 small, trimmed and thinly sliced

Baby plum or cherry tomatoes 4, halved

Chopped basil 4 tbsp

Chopped mint 4 tbsp

Garlic 1 clove, peeled and crushed

Pine nuts 1 tbsp, toasted

Lamb steaks or chops 2, or 4 if small

Butter 15g (½oz)

Nutmeg grated

 Scan the **QR Code** with a smartphone for an ingredients shopping list

To make the mash, put the celeriac and 1 teaspoon lemon juice in a pan, cover with cold water and add a pinch of salt. Bring to the boil, then cover, reduce the heat and simmer for 20–25 minutes until soft.

Meanwhile, make the ratatouille. Heat 1 tablespoon oil in a frying pan over a medium heat. Add the onion and cook for about 5 minutes until softened. Add the fennel and courgette and cook for about 15 minutes until just tender, stirring occasionally. Take the pan off the heat, add the tomato halves and season well.

To make the pesto, mix the herbs in a bowl with the garlic, pine nuts, remaining lemon juice and 2 tablespoons of the oil. Season to taste.

To cook the lamb, heat a griddle or frying pan over a high heat. Brush the meat with the remaining oil and cook for 2 minutes on both sides, then reduce the heat to low and cook for a further 3–4 minutes on each side.

Drain the celeriac when it is soft, return it to the pan and place over a low heat to remove any moisture. Add the butter and mash well. Season well with salt, pepper and nutmeg.

Serve the lamb on the mash on warm plates accompanied with the ratatouille and pesto.

 Cook's TIPS

Keep celeriac in the fridge and use it for roasting in chunks or making into a potato and celeriac soup.

Toast half a bag of pine nuts at a time and keep them in a jar, ready to use in pesto or salads.

Soft and creamy celeriac mash with tender lamb and a colourful ratatouille – all served with a fresh homemade pesto.

Classic pub grub at home. This gorgeous recipe is not only delicious but easy to make too.

Beef Steak with Peppercorn Sauce & Potato Wedges

 Serves 2

Time 1¼ hours
Per portion: 747 Kcal
62g fat (30g saturated)

Preheat the oven to 200°C/400°F/Gas 6. Pour 2 tablespoons oil into a roasting tin and place in the oven to heat up.

Meanwhile, put the potatoes in a pan of water, bring to the boil and simmer for 2 minutes. Drain well and rough up the edges by shaking in the pan.

Remove the roasting tin from the oven and carefully add the wedges. Season with salt and pepper. Using a long handled spoon, coat the potato wedges in the oil and spread out in the tin.

Return the tin to the oven and cook for 45–50 minutes until crisp, turning after 20 minutes.

To make the sauce, heat 2 teaspoons oil in a small heavy-based frying pan over a medium heat. Add the onion and garlic and cook for about 5 minutes until softened, stirring frequently.

Add the peppercorns and 4 tablespoons of the beef stock. Simmer until almost all the liquid has evaporated, then add the leftover stock with the cream and bring to the boil. Simmer until reduced and thickened, stirring occasionally. Season to taste.

For the steaks, preheat a griddle until hot. Brush 1 teaspoon oil onto both sides of the steaks, then cook according to taste. Usually, for rare cook for 2 minutes on each side, for medium cook for 3–4 minutes on each side, and for well done cook for 4–6 minutes on each side. Leave to rest for a few minutes.

Serve the steaks with the potato wedges, salad and the peppercorn sauce.

Olive oil 2 tbsp plus 3 tsp

Potatoes 2, peeled and cut into wedges

Salt and freshly ground black pepper

Onion 1 small, peeled and finely chopped

Garlic 1 clove, peeled and finely chopped

Whole black peppercorns 2 tsp, lightly crushed

Beef stock 150ml (¼ pint)

Double cream 150ml pot

Beef rump steaks 2

Mixed salad 50g packet, to serve

 Scan the **QR Code** with a smartphone for an ingredients shopping list

Fresh Fruit with Chocolate Dip

Serves 1

Time 10 minutes
Per portion: 255 Kcal
11g fat (6g saturated)

Dark chocolate 35g (1½oz), broken into pieces

Milk 1 tbsp

Mixed fruit, such as strawberries, blueberries, blackberries and raspberries 175g (6oz)

Scan the **QR Code** with a smartphone for an ingredients shopping list

Put the chocolate and milk in a heatproof bowl and set it over a pan of barely simmering water. Stir until it has melted, making sure it doesn't overheat.

Remove the pan from the heat and stir to make a smooth thick glossy sauce.

Carefully remove the bowl from the pan and pour the chocolate into a small pot. Serve immediately with the berries to dip into the chocolate sauce.

Supermarkets sell a range of packets of prepared fruit, such as summer fruit grazing trays with pineapple, melon, watermelon, strawberries and mango chunks, or tropical fruit selections, such as pineapple, mango, coconut, papaya and pomegranate.

Simple, yet stunning. The bitterness of the dark chocolate contrasts wonderfully with the sweetness of the fruit.

Wonderfully simple, yet totally delicious; the lemony crème fraîche provides a creamy accompaniment to the roasted strawberries.

Roasted Strawberries with Lemon Ripple

 Serves 1

Time 15 minutes
Per portion: 378 Kcal
31g fat (20g saturated)

Preheat the oven to 220°C/425°F/Gas 7. Spread the strawberries in one layer in a small ovenproof dish. Dot with the butter and sprinkle with the orange zest and juice and the sugar. Roast for 10–12 minutes until soft but still keeping their shape.

Spoon the strawberries and juices into a dish. Gently swirl the lemon curd into the crème fraîche and then spoon into the dish. Serve immediately.

Strawberries 110g (4oz), hulled
Butter 15g (½oz)
Orange 1 tsp grated zest and 1 tbsp juice
Caster sugar 1 tsp
Crème fraîche 3 tbsp
Lemon curd 2 tsp

Scan the **QR Code** with a smartphone for an ingredients shopping list

This pudding is just as delicious if you leave the strawberries to cool after roasting them.

Use the remaining crème fraîche to make a sauce or serve it with another pud or on top of soup.

Ring the changes by using whipped double cream or mascarpone instead of crème fraîche.

Serves 1

Peach & Ginger Pavlova

Time 40 minutes
Per portion: 311 Kcal
5g fat (3g saturated)

Egg white 1
Caster sugar 50g (2oz)
Cornflour ¼ tsp
White wine vinegar ¼ tsp
Plain Greek yogurt 1 tbsp
Chopped glacé ginger 1 tsp
Peach ½, sliced

Scan the **QR Code** with a smartphone for an ingredients shopping list

Preheat the oven to 150°C/300°F/Gas 2 and line a baking sheet with non-stick paper.

Put the egg white into a scrupulously clean bowl and whisk it until it is stiff. Then gradually whisk in the sugar, a teaspoon at a time. Continue whisking until the meringue mixture is thick and glossy.

Mix the cornflour and vinegar together and fold them into the mixture.

Spoon the mixture into two mounds on the baking sheet. Spread each into a circle about 9cm (3¾in) in diameter and make a slight dip in the centre of each.

Cook for 30-35 minutes until the meringue mounds are pale golden and can be peeled off the paper easily. Leave to cool.

Just before serving, put 1 meringue onto a plate (wrap the other and store in the cupboard for another day), spoon the yogurt on top and sprinkle with the chopped ginger. Arrange the peach slices over the yogurt and serve.

Glacé ginger is similar to glacé cherries and can be found in the baking section of the supermarket. If you can't find it, you could use drained and chopped stem ginger.

Use the other peach half chopped into a leafy salad and serve with chicken or add it to a crunchy salad dressed with light mayonnaise.

Crumble the other meringue into Greek yogurt with red berries for an Eton mess-like dessert.

Ginger is an unusual ingredient to use in Pavlova but its fiery taste complements the sweetness of the meringue perfectly.

This delectable dessert is so quick and easy to make, you can enjoy a restaurant-quality pud any or every day of the week!

Lemon Posset

 *Serves 2*

Time 15 minutes plus chilling
Per portion: 943 Kcal
81g fat (50g saturated)

Pour the cream into a saucepan and bring gently to a simmer, stirring occasionally. Add the sugar and stir until dissolved.

Add the lemon juice and bring to the boil, tasting to check the sweetness – you may wish to add a little more lemon juice or sugar as necessary. Simmer for 2 minutes before removing from the heat. Whisk well and then pour the posset into two heatproof glasses.

Leave to cool then chill in the fridge for about 3 hours until set before serving. Top with a few berries if you like.

Double cream 300ml pot
Caster sugar 100g (3½oz)
Lemon 1 large, 2–3 tbsp juice
Fresh berries to serve (optional)

Scan the **QR Code** with a smartphone for an ingredients shopping list

It is better to measure the juice from the lemon so you can easily add as much or as little as you need.

Serves 2

Portuguese Baked Custards

Time 40 minutes
Per portion: 144 Kcal
7g fat (3g saturated)

Grated orange zest 1 tsp
Caster sugar 1 tbsp
Egg 1 plus 1 **egg yolk**
Milk 200ml (7fl oz)
Ground cinnamon a pinch

 Scan the QR Code with a smartphone for an ingredients shopping list

Preheat the oven to 180°C/350°F/Gas 4. Put the orange zest, sugar and egg plus egg yolk into a jug and whisk it with a fork.

Pour the milk into a saucepan, bring it just to the boil and then gradually whisk it into the egg mixture.

Pour this into two ramekin dishes and sprinkle with cinnamon. Put the dishes into a small roasting tin or shallow cake tin and pour enough boiling water into the tin to come halfway up the sides of the dishes.

Cook for 20–25 minutes or until the custards are set. Leave to cool then chill in the fridge before serving.

 You could use lemon zest instead of the orange and grate nutmeg on the top.

A modern twist on the classic baked custard with the simple addition of zesty orange.

A creamy, comforting pudding that is perfect for a chilly evening in front of the fire.

Apricots Baked in Buttermilk Custard

Serves 2

Time 50 minutes
Per portion: 347 Kcal
1g fat (1g saturated)

Preheat the oven to 200°C/400°F/Gas 6. Lightly butter two 300ml (½ pint) gratin dishes. Lay the apricot halves in the base of each dish, cut-side up. Sprinkle with 2 teaspoons of the sugar and then bake for 15–20 minutes until softened.

Whisk the cornflour into the buttermilk with the remaining sugar and the vanilla extract. Pour the mixture into the dishes around the fruit.

Put the dishes into a roasting tin and pour enough boiling water into the tin to come halfway up the sides of the dishes.

Reduce the heat to 160°C/325°F/Gas 3 and bake for 20–25 minutes until the custard is just set but still has a slight wobble. Sprinkle with almonds and icing sugar, if you like, and serve warm or chilled.

Butter for greasing
Apricots 5, halved and pitted
Caster sugar 2 tsp, plus 2 tbsp
Cornflour 2 tsp
Buttermilk 284ml pot
Vanilla extract about ½ tsp
Toasted flaked almonds 1 tbsp (optional)
Icing sugar for dusting (optional)

Scan the **QR Code** with a smartphone for an ingredients shopping list

This is best baked in shallow gratin dishes or in one dish if you prefer.

You could use peach slices instead of the apricots.

 *Serves 2*

Crêpes with Brandy Marmalade Sauce

Time 40 minutes
Per portion: 514 Kcal
20g fat (3g saturated)

Plain flour 50g (2oz)
Caster sugar 25g (1oz)
Egg 1
Semi-skimmed milk 60ml (2fl oz)
Sunflower oil 3–4 tbsp
Marmalade 3 tbsp
Brandy 2 tbsp

 Scan the **QR Code** with a smartphone for an ingredients shopping list

Put the flour, sugar and egg into a bowl and mix. Then mix the milk with 60ml (2fl oz) of water in a jug and gradually whisk it into the sweetened flour and egg, together with 2 tablespoons oil, to make a smooth batter.

Put the marmalade in a small saucepan with the brandy. Bring to the boil, stirring, until the marmalade melts, then boil for a few minutes to make a syrup. Remove the pan from the heat and leave to stand.

Pour a little oil into the base of a small non-stick frying pan. When hot, pour away the excess oil. Add 2 tablespoons of the crêpe mixture to the pan and tilt the pan until the base is covered. Cook for 1–2 minutes until the base is lightly browned.

Turn the crêpe over with a knife and cook the other side. Slide it from the pan and keep warm. Repeat until all the batter has been used.

Arrange the crêpes on warmed plates and spoon the marmalade sauce over them. Serve immediately.

 If you don't have brandy, simply add 2 tbsp water instead.

You could serve the crêpes with a scoop of vanilla ice cream if you like.

With these delicious crêpes, smothered in a tangy brandy sauce, you can imagine you're tucked away in a tiny Parisian cafe.

A fabulous twist on the classic Bakewell tart, these mini tarts taste truly scrumptious with the addition of velvety apricots.

Apricot Bakewell Tarts

 Serves 2

Time 45 minutes plus chilling
Per portion: 546 Kcal
26g fat (8g saturated)

Place the flour and 2 teaspoons sugar in a bowl and rub in the butter to make fine crumbs. Stir in 2-3 teaspoons cold water to make a smooth dough.

Knead lightly on a floured surface and then cut in half and roll each half out thinly. Use to line two 10cm (4in) diameter tart tins. Trim the tops and chill for 15 minutes.

Preheat the oven to 190°C/375°F/Gas 5. Spread the jam over the base of the tarts and then sprinkle with the apricots.

Separate the egg into two medium-sized bowls. Whisk the white until stiff and moist peaks form. Add the remaining sugar and almond extract to the egg yolk and whisk until it is thick and pale. Fold in the ground almonds and milk, then gently fold in the egg white.

Pour the mixture over the apricots, sprinkle with the flaked almonds, if using, and bake for 15–20 minutes until golden and just set. Check after 10 minutes and cover with foil if necessary to stop over-browning.

Leave to cool for 15 minutes, remove from the tins and dust with icing sugar. Serve with fresh cream or ice cream if you like.

Plain flour 50g (2oz)

Caster sugar 2 tsp plus 25g (1oz)

Butter 25g (1oz), diced

Strawberry or raspberry jam 4 tsp

Dried ready-to-eat apricots 40g (1½oz), sliced

Egg 1

Almond extract a few drops

Ground almonds 3 tbsp

Skimmed milk 2 tbsp

Flaked almonds 1 tbsp (optional)

Icing sugar for dusting

Cream or ice cream to serve (optional)

 Scan the **QR Code** with a smartphone for an ingredients shopping list

 You could use other types of dried ready-to-eat fruits. Choose your favourite.

If you don't have individual tart tins, you could use poachette rings set on a baking tray.

 *Serves 2*

Plum Tarts

Time 30 minutes
Per portion: 309 Kcal
15g fat (7g saturated)

Puff pastry 125g (5oz)

Ripe plums 175g (6oz), pitted and thickly sliced

Milk 1 tsp

Redcurrant jelly or strawberry jam 2 tsp, warmed

Icing sugar for dusting

 Scan the **QR Code** with a smartphone for an ingredients shopping list

Preheat the oven to 220°C/425°F/Gas 7. Roll out the pastry on a lightly floured surfaced to a rectangle measuring 20 x 12.5cm (8 x 5in). Cut it into two smaller 10 x 12.5cm (4 x 5in) rectangles.

Put the pastries on a wetted baking sheet. Knock up the edges with the edge of a knife and flute them between your finger and thumb.

Arrange the plum pieces on each pastry slice, leaving a small border. Brush the edges with milk.

Cook for 15–18 minutes or until the pastries are browned. Brush with the jelly or jam, then dust with icing sugar and serve warm.

 Freeze any leftover puff pastry, well wrapped, in portions (unless it has previously been frozen).

For a party dish, you could add a thin layer of marzipan under the plums.

Soft, slightly tart pieces of plum on a crisp pastry base; the perfect mid-afternoon pick-me-up.

A

antipasti pitta pizza 133

Anzac biscuits 98

apples

   apple & mint sorbet 94

   grilled mackerel with hot cabbage salad 17

apricots

   baked in buttermilk custard 165

   Bakewell tarts 169

artichokes

   antipasti pitta pizza 133

   sausage & artichoke rolls 78

asparagus

   hearty kiln-roasted salmon salad 42

   Mozzarella & asparagus baguette 10

aubergines, mini moussakas 149

avocado, baked salmon tricolore 45

B

bacon *see also* pancetta, cheesy bacon mash 77

Bakewell tarts, apricot 169

banana & sultana loaf 114

beans

   pan-fried pork with homemade spicy beans 29

   pappardelle with chorizo-topped cod 14

   sea bass Spanish-style 141

beef

   beef & polenta pies 93

   cheat's beef curry 58

   Cornish pasties 90

   fillet steak with chimichurri sauce 134

   goulash 86

   Italian meatballs 33

   Moroccan mince 85

   roast beef in a Yorkshire pudding 30

   steak with peppercorn sauce & potato wedges 153

   warming beef in beer stew 89

biscuits

   Anzac biscuits 98

   lemon swirl biscuits 97

blueberry & buttermilk muffins 105

bread

   antipasti pitta pizza 133

   Mozzarella & asparagus baguette 10

   pancetta & mushrooms on toast with egg 26

   spiced chicken on a bun 49

broccoli & Stilton quiches 65

bulgur wheat, Thai chicken skewers 50

butter beans

   pan-fried pork with homemade spicy beans 29

   sea bass Spanish-style 141

buttermilk

   apricots baked in buttermilk custard 165

   blueberry & buttermilk muffins 105

   buttermilk & cinnamon scones 106

butternut squash, four veg & ricotta cannelloni 62

C

cabbage, grilled mackerel with hot cabbage salad 17

cakes and bakes *see also* tarts

   banana & sultana loaf 114

   blueberry & buttermilk muffins 105

   buttermilk & cinnamon scones 106

   chocolate fudgey cake 118

   Cornish saffron cake 117

   fruit slices 101

   ginger & prune scones 109

   no-bake chocolate squares 102

   raspberry Swiss roll 113

carrots

   four veg & ricotta cannelloni 62

   Moroccan mince 85

   warming beef in beer stew 89

casseroles

   chicken with thyme & orange 70

   pork & pumpkin 74

cauliflower, creamy monkfish & cauliflower curry 137

celeriac, griddled lamb with fresh pesto, celeriac mash & ratatouille 150

cheat's beef curry 58

cheese

   antipasti pitta pizza 133

   broccoli & Stilton quiches 65

   cheesy bacon mash 77

   goat's cheese & mushroom pizza 41

   griddled Halloumi with wild rocket 34

   Mozzarella & asparagus baguette 10

   mushrooms with goat's cheese 122

   pancetta omelette with pea shoot salad 25

   Parmesan plaice 13

chicken

   chicken & sweet potato with herby sauce 145

   chicken casserole with thyme & orange 70

   chicken escalopes with thyme and courgette 53

   chicken with mushrooms & tarragon 73

   goujons with pea shoot salad 21

   lemon & thyme roast poussin and potatoes 129

   southern-style chicken with oven-baked chips 22

   spiced chicken on a bun 49

   spring chicken in broth with minted pea purée 146

Thai chicken skewers 50

chickpeas, Moroccan mince 85

chimichurri sauce 134

chips, oven-baked 22

chocolate

    chocolate fudgey cake 118

    fresh fruit with chocolate dip 154

    no-bake chocolate squares 102

chorizo

    pappardelle with chorizo-topped cod 14

    sea bass Spanish-style 141

cod, pappardelle with chorizo-topped cod 14

Cornish pasties 90

Cornish saffron cake 117

courgettes

    chicken escalopes with thyme and courgette 53

    four veg & ricotta cannelloni 62

    griddled lamb with fresh pesto, celeriac mash & ratatouille 150

    sea bass Spanish-style 141

couscous, romano peppers stuffed with fruity couscous 37

crêpes with brandy marmalade sauce 166

curry

    cheat's beef 58

    creamy monkfish & cauliflower 137

    prawn & mango 46

custards

    apricots baked in buttermilk custard 165

    Portuguese baked 162

D

desserts & puddings *see also* tarts

    apricots baked in buttermilk custard 165

    crêpes with brandy marmalade sauce 166

    fresh fruit with chocolate dip 154

    lemon posset 161

    peach & ginger pavlova 158

    Portuguese baked custards 162

    roasted strawberries with lemon ripple 157

E

eggs

    crêpes with brandy marmalade sauce 166

    hearty kiln-roasted salmon salad 42

    pancetta & mushrooms on toast with egg 26

    pancetta omelette with pea shoot salad 25

    peach & ginger pavlova 158

    Portuguese baked custards 162

    stir-fried pork with egg-fried rice 54

F

fennel, griddled lamb with fresh pesto, celeriac mash & ratatouille 150

fillet steak with chimichurri sauce 134

fish

    baked salmon tricolore 45

    creamy monkfish & cauliflower curry 137

    golden-topped fish pies 66

    hearty kiln-roasted salmon salad 42

    pan-fried sea bass & scallops with Hollandaise sauce 138

    pappardelle with chorizo-topped cod 14

    Parmesan plaice 13

    sea bass Spanish-style 141

    Thai fishcakes with crunchy salad 69

fruit, fresh, with chocolate dip 154

fruit slices 101

G

ginger

    ginger & prune scones 109

    gingery prawn stir-fry 142

    peach & ginger pavlova 158

goat's cheese

    goat's cheese & mushroom pizza 41

    mushrooms with goat's cheese 122

golden-topped fish pies 66

goulash, beef 86

H

Halloumi, griddled, with wild rocket 34

I

Italian meatballs 33

K

kale, sea bass Spanish-style 141

L

lamb

    braised, with lemon & parsnips 82

    griddled, with fresh pesto, celeriac mash & ratatouille 150

    mini moussakas 149

    Moroccan mince 85

    spicy lamb with creamy mash 57

lemons

    lemon & thyme roast poussin and potatoes 129

    lemon posset 161

    lemon swirl biscuits 97

lentils, Moroccan mince 85

M

mackerel, grilled, with hot cabbage salad 17

mango, prawn & mango curry 46

monkfish, creamy monkfish & cauliflower curry 137

Moroccan mince 85

moussakas, mini 149

Mozzarella & asparagus baguette 10

muffins, blueberry & buttermilk 105

mushrooms

    chicken with mushrooms & tarragon 73

    goat's cheese & mushroom pizza 41

    mushrooms with goat's cheese 122

    pancetta & mushrooms on toast with egg 26

N

no-bake chocolate squares 102

noodles

    gingery prawn stir-fry 142

    vegetable chow mein 38

O

oats, Anzac biscuits 98

oranges, chicken casserole with thyme & orange 70

P

pancakes, crêpes with brandy marmalade sauce 166

pancetta

    pancetta & mushrooms on toast with egg 26

    pancetta omelette with pea shoot salad 25

pappardelle with chorizo-topped cod 14

Parmesan plaice 13

parsnips

    braised lamb with lemon & parsnips 82

    Moroccan mince 85

pasta

    four veg & ricotta cannelloni 62

    Italian meatballs 33

    pappardelle with chorizo-topped cod 14

    prawn cocktail pasta 125

pavlova, peach & ginger 158

pea shoots

    chicken goujons with pea shoot salad 21

    pancetta omelette with pea shoot salad 25

peach & ginger pavlova 158

peas, spring chicken in broth with minted pea purée 146

peppers

    beef goulash 86

    romano peppers stuffed with fruity couscous 37

    sea bass Spanish-style 141

pesto, fresh 150

pies

    beef & polenta pies 93

    Cornish pasties 90

    golden-topped fish pies 66

pizza

    antipasti pitta 133

    goat's cheese & mushroom 41

plum tarts 170

polenta, beef & polenta pies 93

pork

    pan-fried pork with homemade spicy beans 29

    pork & pumpkin casserole 74

    pork parcels 130

    stir-fried pork with egg-fried rice 54

Portuguese baked custards 162

posset, lemon 161

potatoes

    beef steak with peppercorn sauce & potato wedges 153

    cheesy bacon mash 77

    Cornish pasties 90

    golden-topped fish pies 66

    lemon & thyme roast poussin and potatoes 129

    oven-baked chips 22

    spicy lamb with creamy mash 57

    spring chicken in broth with minted pea purée 146

potted shrimps 18

prawns

    gingery prawn stir-fry 142

    prawn & mango curry 46

    prawn cocktail pasta 125

prunes, ginger & prune scones 109

pumpkin, pork & pumpkin casserole 74

Q

quiche, broccoli & Stilton 65

quinoa, Thai chicken skewers 50

R

raspberry Swiss roll 113

ratatouille, with griddled lamb, fresh pesto & celeriac mash 150

red cabbage, grilled mackerel with hot cabbage salad 17

rice, stir-fried pork with egg-fried rice 54

rocket, griddled Halloumi with wild rocket 34

romano peppers stuffed with fruity couscous 37

S

salads
- chicken goujons with pea shoots 21
- griddled Halloumi with wild rocket 34
- hearty kiln-roasted salmon 42
- pancetta omelette with pea shoots 25
- Thai fishcakes with crunchy salad 69

salmon
- baked salmon tricolore 45
- hearty kiln-roasted salmon salad 42
- Thai fishcakes with crunchy salad 69

samphire, pan-fried sea bass & scallops with Hollandaise sauce 138

sandwiches
- Mozzarella & asparagus baguette 10
- spiced chicken on a bun 49

sauces
- brandy marmalade 166
- chimichurri 134
- chocolate dip 154
- garlicky tomato 81
- herby 145
- peppercorn 153
- pesto 150

sausages
- sausage & artichoke rolls 78
- spinach sausages with garlicky tomato sauce 81

scallops
- pan-fried sea bass & scallops with Hollandaise sauce 138
- speedy spicy scallops 126

scones
- buttermilk & cinnamon 106
- ginger & prune 109

sea bass
- pan-fried with scallops & Hollandaise sauce 138
- Spanish-style 141

seafood
- gingery prawn stir-fry 142
- pan-fried sea bass & scallops with Hollandaise sauce 138
- potted shrimps 18
- prawn & mango curry 46
- prawn cocktail pasta 125
- speedy spicy scallops 126

shrimps, potted 18

sorbet, apple & mint 94

southern-style chicken with oven-baked chips 22

spinach
- four veg & ricotta cannelloni 62
- sea bass Spanish-style 141
- spinach sausages with garlicky tomato sauce 81

steak
- beef steak with peppercorn sauce & potato wedges 153
- fillet steak with chimichurri sauce 134

strawberries, roasted, with lemon ripple 157

sweet potatoes
- chicken & sweet potato with herby sauce 145
- golden-topped fish pies 66
- southern-style chicken with oven-baked chips 22

Swiss roll, raspberry 113

T

tarts
- apricot Bakewell tarts 169
- broccoli & Stilton quiches 65
- plum tarts 170
- sticky walnut tart 110

Thai chicken skewers 50

Thai fishcakes with crunchy salad 69

tomatoes
- baked salmon tricolore 45
- beef goulash 86
- cheat's beef curry 58
- four veg & ricotta cannelloni 62
- griddled lamb with fresh pesto, celeriac mash & ratatouille 150
- Italian meatballs 33
- mini moussakas 149
- Moroccan mince 85
- Mozzarella & asparagus baguette 10
- pan-fried pork with homemade spicy beans 29
- pappardelle with chorizo-topped cod 14
- spinach sausages with garlicky tomato sauce 81

V

vegetables *see also* salads; *specific vegetables*
- chow mein 38
- four veg & ricotta cannelloni 62
- gingery prawn stir-fry 142
- stir-fried pork with egg-fried rice 54

W

walnuts, sticky walnut tart 110

Thanks to

Executive Editor	Nick Rowe
Managing Editor	Emily Davenport
Editor	Emma Callery
Photographer	Steve Lee
Food Stylist	Sara Lewis
Props Stylist	Olivia Wardle
Recipes created by	Lucy Knox, Sara Lewis and Kate Moseley
Proof Reader	Aune Butt
Indexer	Ruth Ellis
Nutritional Consultant	Paul McArdle
Recipe Testers	Richard Davenport
	Katy Hackforth
	Jo Kilgour
	Claire Nadin
	Anne-Marie Neild
	Lucy Padget
	Karen Perry
	Laura Pickering
	Gudrun Waskett
Production	Cath Linter

Eaglemoss Consumer Publications Ltd
Electra House, Electra Way, Crewe, Cheshire, CW1 6GL
Tel 01270 270050
www.dairydiary.co.uk
www.dairydiarychat.co.uk

First printed May 2015
© Eaglemoss Consumer Publications Ltd
ISBN: 978-0-9571772-7-7
123456789

All rights reserved. No part of this publication may be reproduced, transmitted, or stored in a retrieval system, in any form or by any means, without permission in writing from Eaglemoss Consumer Publications Ltd.

Whilst every care has been taken in compiling the information in this book, the publishers cannot accept responsibility for any errors, in advertent or not, that may be found or may occur at some time in the future owing to changes in legislation or for any other reason.